Ministry Across Cultures:
Sharing the Christian Faith in Asia

Series Preface

Regnum Studies in Mission are born from the lived experience of Christians and Christian communities in mission, especially but not solely in the fast growing churches among the poor of the world. These churches have more to tell than stories of growth. They are making significant impacts on their cultures in the cause of Christ. They are producing 'cultural products' which express the reality of Christian faith, hope and love in their societies.

Regnum Studies in Mission are the fruit often of rigorous research to the highest international standards and always of authentic Christian engagement in the transformation of people and societies. And these are for the world. The formation of Christian theology, missiology and practice in the twenty-first century will depend to a great extent on the active participation of growing churches contributing biblical and culturally appropriate expressions of Christian practice to inform World Christianity.

Series Editors

A full listing of titles in this series
appears at the end of this book

Much has been written along the lines of theoretical and theological perspectives on the relationship between the gospel and culture. The value of this book is that it goes beyond such discussions to deal with practical implications grounded in several Asian contexts. The contributors are experienced practitioners of ministry in Asia and offer very helpful insights and examples of the kind of issues encountered in being pastors and teachers and doing ministry across cultures. They question unexamined assumptions and habits found in those who try to do ministry in another culture without adequate study, reflection and understanding.

This book is, therefore, useful for missionaries, evangelists, tent-makers, theological educators and church leaders. It is in fact useful for all Christians living in a world where local realities are no longer mono-cultural.

Dr. Robert Solomon (formerly Bishop of the Methodist Church of Singapore)

The 21st century has introduced new challenges for communicating the gospel particularly in burgeoning places of urbanization on all continents especially in Asia. Those who minister in such places are the authors of this "intermediate level text on contextualization." The topic of contextualization of the gospel is critical since it is never straightforward and there are always lessons to be learned. Therefore the reflections, examples, and missiological foundations presented from a variety of authors will be helpful to anyone called to minister in similar situations.

Kirk Franklin, Executive Director, Wycliffe Global Alliance

In recent years the subject of contextualisation has been a prominent topic among mission workers and missiologists. The debate has focused on how far we can go in contextualising the Gospel. When does it begin to tip over into syncretism? Some have pushed the boundaries of contextualisation far and this has caused considerable concern in certain circles. There has been an intensive debate going on between some mission agencies and denominations in the USA on this important subject.

Around 7 years ago I set up a study group in SIM which worked for 9 months to consider contextualisation of the Gospel especially in relation to one of the world's major religions. It also considered translation guidelines for the mission. This was a very important exercise for us and has helped guide our teams around the world in various contexts. I welcome OMF's commitment to this important subject with the publication of *Mission Across Cultures – Sharing the Christian Faith in Asia.*

Malcolm McGregor, former SIM International Director, 2003 to 2013, currently on the staff at Carrubbers Christian Centre, Edinburgh

The issue of contextualization lies at the heart of mission in every situation without exception. I rejoice therefore in this book as a significant contribution to this debate. It is my prayer that God's people in every continent and country may be encouraged in the application of contextualization principles both personally and in their church.

Martin Goldsmith, Author and Associate Lecturer
All Nations Christian College, Ware, UK

Ministry Across Cultures:
Sharing the Christian Faith in Asia

Edited by Warren R. Beattie

First published 2016 by Regnum Books International

Regnum is an imprint of the Oxford Centre for Mission Studies
St. Philip and St. James Church
Woodstock Road
Oxford OX2 6HR, UK
www.ocms.ac.uk/regnum

09 08 07 06 05 04 03 7 6 5 4 3 2 1

British Library Cataloguing in Publication Data
A catalogue record for this book is available from the British Library

ISBN: 978-1-908355-99-7

Typeset by Words by Design

Printed and bound by CPI Group (UK) Ltd, Croydon, CR0 4YY

DEDICATED TO

Stroma
Francis

CONTENTS

PREFACE

Ministry Across Cultures looks at the issues that arise when engaging in ministry in different cultural contexts across Asia. It forms part of a much larger discussion about contextualization and contextual theology as they relate to Asia. What is distinctive about this book is the concern to focus on the practical elements of this discussion whilst connecting them to theory in a way that will stimulate practitioners to think further about the implications of culture on their ministry.

The idea for writing this book started with some papers and presentations that were shared at a Mission Research Consultation (MRC) in 2004, which brought together researchers, educators, leaders and practitioners within the mission community. As we considered a number of issues in Asia, we were conscious that the topic of "ministry in Asian contexts" could be explored further. We decided to focus on a few core areas of ministry – evangelism, discipleship, the life of the church and teaching in church. To set these in context, we decided to introduce the ideas of culture and worldview with examples relating to Asia and to conclude with some reflection on the implications of culture for leaders who engage in ministry in Asian contexts.

Bibliography and Readings

There is a tension in writing about Asian contexts and contextual theology using English rather than local Asian languages. We have tried to represent a spectrum of writers and thinkers – some from Asia and some from elsewhere – and we hope that the kind of materials and authors that we are suggesting will lead readers to materials connected more specifically to their cultures of interest, including those in local languages.

Although we have made every effort to include the most recent and relevant materials, readers will notice that some books date back one or two decades or even further. Especially in the area of culture, discussions that come from an earlier era are often surprisingly readable in today's context. We might note particularly Eugene Nida's books in this regard; of the other authors included, there is one other earlier book, cited by many of the chapter contributors, that deserves a special mention – *Anthropological Insights for Missionaries* – Paul Hiebert's introductory guide to culture for missionaries. This is an accessible, thoughtful and practical book that deserves to be widely read, with its interest in connecting theory and practice and the author's clear and simple style revealing a wealth of insight and experience.

In the chapters, we have devised a number of categories to highlight books of interest: "Book Idea" (a recent book which connects to the core theme of the chapter); "Suggested reading" (which indicates basic treatments of a subject) and "Further reading" (which offers a wider range of materials); for those interested in greater detail, more exhaustive references are found in the notes and the bibliography. Three dictionaries cited in the bibliography – the *Dictionary of Mission Theology*, the *Global Dictionary of Theology* and *A Dictionary of Asian Christianity* – would all contain information about mission and ministry in Asia which would be of interest to readers of this book. We have deliberately not included a great deal of literature on "missional church" (in English) as its point of reference tends to be Europe, Australasia or north America – our approach has been rather to look at a range of issues affecting the church, ministry and mission in their Asian settings as a more fruitful way of understanding the "missional church" in Asian contexts – those wishing to explore further the existing bibliography on this topic should see Van Gelder and Zscheile's *The Missional Church in Perspective*.

Contributors to This and Other Research Projects

We would like to express our thanks to the following people for their help at various stages with this project:

To the Mission Research Department (MRD) Team – to Steven Wolf and Kimberley Goh for their many contributions to the MRD including this project, and especially for their help in bringing together materials for the initial proposal of the *Missional Church in Asian Contexts* Series.

To colleagues who have been involved in the process from project to published book – Ramon Rocha has given invaluable advice at various stages of the process with his excellent knowledge of books and the world of publishing; Jennie Fung has helped us to think about how Mission Research Media projects connect to other aspects of OMF Publishing; Clare Cox, Einar and Annelies Wilder-Smith have given information about publishing for different continents. As the person responsible for the management of Training and Research within OMF International, Patrick Fung has both welcomed and contributed to more extended reflection on mission and has encouraged projects like this one to be part of the agency's contribution to the wider missional community. David and Rosemary Harley were part of a small group with a focus on Contextualization from the MRC in 2004 and have helped to set this project on its way following discussions in 2007. The colleagues who have formed a Council of Reference to the Research Department, the late Chua How Chuang, Yuzo Imamura, Roger Senior and Anne Ruck, have all contributed to this, and similar projects, in a variety of ways; the final member, Rose Dowsett has given advice and encouragement at many stages along the way, especially in relation to publishing, and has helped with a number of practical matters. And also to Derek Beattie for help with proof-reading in the final stages.

To all the writers – Les Taylor, Phil Nicholson, Daniel D. Kim, Minho Song, Melville Szto, David Harley and Brian Michell – for their willingness to connect together again after the MRC (2004) and for their persistence and patience in responding to requests for information over the months, and the years (!) involved in bringing this project to its fruition. Similarly, we are grateful to all the participants at MRC events, who have given of their time and energy and whose insights and collaboration have shaped, informed and enlivened the discussion of mission and the missional church in Asian contexts over the years.

Warren would like to say a special thank you to Karen (who has been with him during six years of work in Singapore with the MRD) for her help and moral support for the whole project and for her advice and creativity regarding the interplay of graphics and text; and also for the extra work involved in being an intermediary with the publishers, after he had relocated to Scotland. Karen and I are also grateful to our spouses, Francis and Stroma, for their support in this, as in so many other projects, that we have been engaged in over the years.

Missional Church in Asian Contexts – Series

In 2012, looking back on three MRC events (with a fourth planned for 2013), we have realized that there is the possibility of sharing further our reflections on a number of themes that connect mission and the church in Asia: these have included wholistic mission, trends and issues in mission, mission and the spirit worlds of Asia and a more intense reflection on the nature of the church. We hope to turn our attention to these in due course, as part of a Series of books entitled – *Missional Church in Asian Contexts* (see the introduction to this Series at the end of the book).

Warren R. Beattie and Karen L. K. Quek
All Nations, Ware, U.K. and Singapore, August 2015

FOREWORD

In his vision of the heavenly city, John noted that the "glory and honour of the nations will be brought into it" and quickly added that "nothing impure will ever enter into it" (Rev. 21:26-27). When these statements are taken together we can appreciate the point about how the Gospel redeems cultures (for the root Greek word that is translated as nations is *ethne*, that is, ethnic groups) so much so that the nations will walk by the light of the heavenly city (Rev. 21:24).

Another way of understanding this vision is to say that there is one biblical gospel but many Christian cultures. Or that the life of Christ is to be incarnated into all cultures as believers live out their faith in their own cultural contexts. The question, though, is how this can be done in a global situation where Christian thoughts, values and practices are largely developed in the West (where Christianity found its main home over a considerable length of its history) and exported to the rest. This is generally still the case even though the centre of gravity of global Christianity, at least in terms of numbers, has shifted from the West to the rest.

Much has been written along the lines of theoretical and theological perspectives on the relationship between the gospel and culture. The value of this book is that it goes beyond such discussions to deal with practical implications grounded in several Asian contexts. The contributors are experienced practitioners of ministry in Asia, and offer very helpful insights and examples of the kind of issues encountered in being pastors and teachers and doing ministry across cultures. They question unexamined assumptions and habits found in those who try to do ministry in another culture without adequate study, reflection and understanding.

This book is, therefore, useful for missionaries, evangelists, tent-makers, theological educators and church leaders. It is in fact useful for all Christians living in a world where local realities are no longer mono-cultural. In many parts of Asia today, one can find people from different parts of the world, thanks to migrant workers and the growing mobility of people across nations. The lessons and insights in this book are relevant to most Christians who now live in multicultural milieus.

The book begins by looking at fundamental issues such as the nature of culture and its relationship to the gospel, and the importance of understanding worldviews and their role in producing deep and lasting Christian transformation. Then the book moves to practice, looking at such issues as culturally relevant and effective evangelism, discipling, church planting, leadership development and theological education. In so doing, the authors encourage careful study of host cultures, and by implication careful study of biblical Christianity and spirituality. Much of popular understanding of what the Bible actually teaches is often confused with

Western forms of thought and practice and needs to be re-examined. The living water must not be confused with the cup so that it can be offered in other culturally relevant cups. In so doing, we are also cautioned by the authors against uncritical cultural adaptation that would result in syncretism or diminish the prophetic and counter-cultural dimensions of the radical message of the Bible and the unique life of Christ.

Cultures are not static and change constantly, and a "pure culture" may not be a reality any longer in our globalised world. The issues highlighted in this book will therefore continue to be explored as contexts change and become more complex – it is an ongoing work this side of eternity. This book will help Christians carry out this important work, and for this reason I am glad that it has been written. It should be widely read and discussed.

Dr. Robert Solomon
(former Bishop of the Methodist Church of Singapore)

INTRODUCTION

Warren R. Beattie

"Culture" is one of the buzzwords of our age but as a term it conjures up a bewildering range of nuances and meanings. Christians live in the midst of cultures and their lives and thinking are shaped by culture. A recent book[1] on *Everyday Theology* has drawn attention to the way in which our lives interact with popular culture: it reminds us, that as contemporary Christians, we need to engage with culture and not allow ourselves to be moulded by our contexts without paying attention to what is going on around us. We need to think about how we live in relation to culture, and how we analyze and respond to cultural activities around us – in short, we need to engage in "everyday theology." This is a challenging but necessary task for Christians who want to understand their world and relate the gospel to it.

Culture and Cultures

Culture embraces more than just the concerns of either popular or highbrow culture: each society is shaped by geography and climate and develops objects, artefacts and physical environments for everyday life; "culture"[2] includes the ideas and values that people hold in a society and how these are worked out in patterns of behaviour. Living in our own familiar cultural settings, we are conscious that we have to make the gospel relevant to the world around us. For Christians who have gone to live and work in other societies, the need to reflect about culture takes on an increased relevance. In the twentieth century, there has been a great deal of reflection about the way in which the gospel is conceptualised in relation to culture – both in terms of its origins in the cultural world of the bible, and in the processes of communicating it to other cultures. Thinkers and practitioners alike, have explored how to share the Christian gospel, and have developed models of the church that dovetail into different cultures. They have also pondered what it means for Christian workers to live and function in a new culture as they proclaim the gospel and engage in ministry.

---

[1] Kevin Vanhoozer, C. A. Anderson and M.J. Sleasman (eds.), *Everyday Theology: How to Read Cultural Texts and Interpret Trends* (Grand Rapids, Michigan: Baker Academic, 2007).

[2] Paul Hiebert, *Anthropological Insights for Missionaries* (Grand Rapids, Michigan: Baker, 1985), 30; see also chapter 1 of this volume.

Contextualisation and the Contemporary Church

People from totally different backgrounds have reflected about culture from the perspective of their own professional training: anthropologists have studied how different societies would shape the way in which the concepts of Christian faith relate to different communities; linguists have looked at how the bible is translated, interpreted and understood by people speaking different languages; and theologians have considered how systems of faith are transmitted across cultural boundaries. As part of this discussion, the term contextualisation was developed, in the early nineteen seventies, to help define the process and so enable people to reflect more clearly on this interplay between culture and theology.[3] Since that time there has been an increased focus on this boundary between theology and contexts and numerous materials on contextualisation have been published.[4] Not that this is simply a modern discussion, since the tensions between Jewish and Gentile Christians described in Acts 15, Christians down through the centuries and throughout the history of the church, have wrestled with how concepts at the heart of their faith are translated into different communities and their cultures.

Contextualization –
Connecting a Universal Story and Every Local Culture

Contextualisation is the task of making the gospel of Jesus Christ real and vivid in each and every cultural context. It tries to encourage each local church to find a "… relevant living theology for their situations." In contextualization, there is an interaction between Christian faith and the character of each specific cultural context: "Authentic contextualisation begins with what God has already done in the story of Israel, and supremely in the story of Jesus Christ. This is the overarching story that must illumine all other stories within a context or culture."[5] The church in each culture needs to take up "the story" of the gospel in such a way that it becomes *their* story.

Contextualisation recognizes that Christian faith needs to be expressed in specific cultural expressions in every generation: it represents a dialogue

---

[3] Shoki Coe, "Contexualising Theology," in *Third World Theologies,* edited by G.H. Anderson, and T. E. Stransky (Grand Rapids, MI: Eerdmans, 1973), 19-24.
[4] The term "contextualization" was developed primarily within Protestant circles. Different branches of the church tend to use terms such as "local theology" or "inculturation," slightly different terms to relate to the same concepts. Other terms which have been used include "accommodation," "indigenization" and so on. For helpful discussion on terms and concepts see Dean Flemming, *Contextualization in the New Testament* (Downers Grove, IL: Inter Varsity Press, 2005), 18-20 and Hwa Yung, *Mangoes or Bananas (*Regnum: Oxford, 1997), 10-14 and 62-76.
[5] I. Tuwere, "What is Contextual Theology: a View from Oceania?" *Pacific Journal of Theology* Series 2 (27) 2002: 7-19.

between the Christian message and individual cultures. The process of contextualisation involves Christian theologians, a local Christian community and an analysis of existing cultural expressions of Christian faith. The Christian message must be lived out, not simply expressed in ideas – it has to be "incarnate" in churches in the non-western world. To engage in contextualisation is to go beyond abstract thinking and the external forms of Christian worship – authentic contextualisation is about "transformed lives" rather than just a quest for "transformed liturgies." [6] This is a two-way process which involves "the contextualisation of Christian faith into a culture" and the "Christianization of culture."

Contextualisation and Practical Ministry

In this book, the authors address how to develop a theology that is genuinely contextual for Christians and churches in Asia as they engage in ministry. The book will emphasize three things: the need for contextualisation to include a practical focus on the sorts of issues that Christians encounter in everyday situations; the idea that contextualisation extends beyond theory to the practicalities of Christian ministry; and the way in which different contexts require different approaches to contextualisation in Asia.

BOOK IDEA

> Chew, Jim. *When You Cross Cultures*. (2nd ed.) Singapore: Nav Media, 2009.

A very practical guide to the issues that people face when they cross cultures to engage in ministry. It surveys the stresses and strains of cross-cultural living; it also makes suggestions about what individuals can do to prepare before moving into a new culture. The author offers a thoughtful discussion about culture and contextualization that raises many of the questions that need to be addressed but does so in a way that is engaging and accessible. A good general introduction to the kind of topics covered in the present volume.

---

[6] Contemporary reflections on culture that consider contextualization include Charles Kraft, *Christianity in Culture* (Rev. ed.) (Maryknoll, N.Y.: Orbis Books, 2004); Robert Schreiter, *Constructing Local Theologies* (Maryknoll, NY: Orbis, 1986); Clemens Sedmak, *Doing Local Theology* (Maryknoll, N.Y.: Orbis Books), 2003; and Dean Flemming, *Contextualization in the New Testament: Patterns for Theology and Mission* (Downers Grove, IL: Intervarsity Press, 2005). For an important review of models see Stephen Bevans, *Models of Contextual Theology* (Maryknoll, N.Y.: Orbis, 2002); for a creative and practical introduction see Anthony Gittins, *Ministry at the Margins: Strategy and Spirituality for Mission* (Maryknoll, N.Y.: Orbis Books, 2002).

Many writers on contextualisation deal with issues of theory or the "development of models" which can be applied to a range of situations. The motivation behind this book was to move beyond the important foundation that these people offer, and to look at the more practical issues that face Christian workers who work in other cultures. Such a study is helpful for practitioners who have moved into a new culture but it is also helpful for those who would like to understand better the nature of mission and who would like to explore the challenges that are involved in cross-cultural ministry. The writers in this volume come from different continents – from Europe, Australasia, North America, and Asia, but they have had the common experience of working in cross-cultural ministry. They have all spent considerable periods of time in Asian countries and have experience living and working in specific cultures using local Asian languages.[7]

An Overview of the Book

Although the focus of the book is about practical ministry, it begins with two important themes that underpin any thinking about contextualisation. The first section of the book introduces culture and worldview. The chapter on culture explores concepts of culture and their implications for ministry. It suggests that culture is pervasive, ever-changing and must be taken into account when engaging in ministry. The chapter on worldview looks at how each culture is shaped by shared ideas and concepts; it explores how to assess worldview and looks at the implications of worldview for contextual ministry.

The central section of the book surveys key areas of ministry: these include core activities such as evangelism, discipleship, the communal life of the church and teaching the bible. These chapters look at different stages of Christian life and ministry and explore how the process of contextualisation relates to each stage. The chapters draw on themes that need to be negotiated to do effective ministry in selected countries in East Asia such as Japan, Thailand, and the Philippines. The chapter on teaching the bible looks at issues encountered across South East Asia. Recognizing that no two contexts in Asia are exactly the same, these chapters explore some of the concrete problems that are encountered doing Christian ministry in Asia.

The final section of the book looks at how contextualization needs to be embraced and developed by leaders of the church in Asia and how it should influence the pastoral ministry of the church in Malaysia; it also considers how lessons learned from one model of contextual training in a multicultural community (in South East Asia) could be applied more

---

[7] With the exception of Dr. David Harley who has, however, had experience of working in Amarhic in Africa; his work in Asia was based in Singapore where English is the medium for "work" – including church life and education.

generally to theological training for students from different cultural backgrounds.

Further Reading on Contextualization

Dowsett, Rose (ed). *Global Mission: Reflections and Case studies.* Pasadena, CA: William Carey Library, 2011.

Flemming, Dean. *Contextualization in the New Testament: Patterns for Theology and Mission.* Downers Grove, IL: Intervarsity Press, 2005.

Hiebert Paul. *Anthropological Insights for Missionaries.* Grand Rapids, Michigan: Baker, 1985.

Schreiter, Robert. *Constructing Local Theologies.* Maryknoll, NY: Orbis, 1986.

Vanhoozer, Kevin (ed.) *Everyday Theology: How to Read Cultural Texts and Interpret Trends.* Grand Rapids, Michigan: Baker Academic, 2007.

PART ONE

CULTURE, WORLDVIEW AND MINISTRY

CULTURE AND CONTEXTUALIZATION

Les Taylor

Les Taylor reminds us that as we build God's church, we must engage with culture conscious of three things: 1) God is involved in every culture; 2) there is no "culture-less" church; and that 3) no culture remains "static." He draws from current understandings of culture and from biblical examples – in particular, the attitude of the first cross-cultural communicators of the early church, as recorded in the book of Acts. He looks to anthropology to help cross-cultural workers be self-aware about their own cultures and how these cultures will shape their understanding of the gospel. With greater self-awareness, they will be better able to interpret other local cultures and to share creatively and contextually what God has done in Jesus Christ.

A realization of the importance of culture has grown over the eight years in which I have lived as a Christian in a South-East Asian community. My thinking has changed over time, largely through my practical experiences of ministry. Theological education has certainly helped me by providing me with a range of tools which, with practice, have enabled me to read and apply God's live-giving text to church contexts. Nevertheless, when it came to real-life ministry and the work of developing a church, I felt like an apprentice who had been taught to make pre-fabricated churches but found himself in a situation where the materials did not seem to fit!

The Church-Builder and Local Materials

Imagine, if you will, a literal "church-builder" who moves to a new location and context. Here, all the buildings are perched on mountainsides – there are no level sites. Bamboo, coconut wood, and coconut thatch are plentiful but there is no pine wood or corrugated iron. Rope is cheap and readily available but nails are expensive, of limited sizes, and inferior quality. Woven bamboo panels can be purchased everywhere but the local hardware store has no particle boards. Local roofing materials require roofs to be steeper than at home, and the climate, with high levels of daily heat and humidity, requires them to be higher in any case, for reasons of ventilation. Faced with these changes in physical context, the church-builder would soon find that they change their approach to putting up church buildings.

The Christian who engages in ministry in a different culture, will find that developing a church for people with different cultural backgrounds requires the same shift in understanding as that experienced by the church-builder described above. After all, the New Testament describes churches as being built with "living stones!"[1] Studying cultural anthropology has really helped me to have a different mindset when it comes to ministry. I have acquired tools and learned approaches that can be applied to churches in different contexts and settings. I have found that when living in a new context (and working with people who are shaped by this culture) the differences in culture mean that there has to be a new approach to developing churches – and many aspects of my understanding of church have had to change. In this chapter, I will discuss the concept of "culture" and show its significance for cross-cultural ministry. I want to offer a few reflections about culture for Christian workers, emphasizing three dimensions in particular: *God is involved in culture*; *there is no 'culture-less' church*; and finally the reality that *cultures are not 'static.'*

The Concept of Culture

The idea of culture is a relatively recent construct, originating in 18th century Europe[2] and a renewed interest in culture among theologians may be related to the vibrant growth of indigenous Christianity in the non-western world.[3] Charles Matthews describes "culture" as the human science's "Swiss Army knife" – a concept with "ambiguities, marked by fluidity, complex inter-relatedness, and incompleteness."[4] He is making the point that the concept itself, like a Swiss Army knife, does *many* things – though *none* particularly well. An anthropologist has summarized earlier definitions of culture to conceive culture as "a coherent set of *ideas, created, shared, transmitted by a group,* which enable them to *make sense of, and cope,* in their (natural and social) world."[5]

---

[1] See 1 Pet 2:4-5.
[2] Those wishing to survey Christian thinking about culture can consult the following books: Charles Kraft, *Anthropology for Christian Witness* (Maryknoll, NY: Orbis, 1996); K. Tanner, *Theories of Culture: a New Agenda for Theology* (Minneapolis: Fortress Press, 1997); Lucien Legrand, *The Bible on Culture* (Maryknoll, N.Y.: Orbis Books, 2000); and Timothy J. Gorringe, *Furthering Humanity: a Theology of Culture* (Aldershot: Ashgate, 2004).
[3] Yao-Hwa E. Sung, "Culture and Hermeneutics," in *Dictionary for Theological Interpretation of the Bible,* ed. by K. J. Vanhoozer et al (Grand Rapids, MI: Baker Academic, 2005), 150. For writings on the non-western world see Lamin O. Sanneh,*Whose Religion is Christianity? The Gospel beyond the West* (Grand Rapids, MI: Eerdmans, 2003) and Philip Jenkins, *The Next Christendom: The Coming of Global Christianity* (Rev. and ex. ed.) (Oxford: Oxford University Press, 2007).
[4] C.T. Matthews, "Culture," In *The Blackwell Companion to Modern Theology,* ed. by G. Jones (Malden, MA ; Oxford, UK: Blackwell, 2004), 48,54. See also Legrand, *The Bible on Culture*, xiii; and Tanner, *Theories of Culture*.
[5] Charles R. Taber, *The World is too Much with Us: "Culture" in Modern Protestant Missions* (Macon: Mercer, 1991), 2-3.

Culture has been conceived as a complex whole that is learned, and shared – including everything that people do, say, have, and think. Various writers have offered glimpses of how difficult it is to explain the exact nature of culture. As a keen observer of human societies, Clifford Geertz speaks of culture as "a web of significance in which humankind is suspended"; writing at the end of the 20ᵗʰ century, the theologian Kathryn Tanner speaks of culture being made up of the meaningful and ordered dimensions of social life, while for Kevin Vanhoozer, culture is everything humans do voluntarily – as opposed to involuntarily![6]

Culture informs how people live their lives and it has an impact on the shared set of assumptions that people develop concerning "the way things are" which is commonly referred to as worldview.[7]

Three Dimensions of Culture

As Christian workers, who engage in ministry across cultures, we need to bring the authoritative text of God's word to the different contexts of the world as we seek to build God's church. As I have reflected on my own personal discovery of culture's importance in the cross-cultural communication of what God has done in Christ, I would like to draw out some of the practical implications of the three dimensions of cultures outlined above for others engaged in ministry.

God is involved in culture

We need to remember that the creator God is involved in culture. Those who assume that the creator God is *not* involved in culture need to think again and think more biblically about their conception of culture. Gailyn Van Rheenen argues that the idea of a separation between the natural and the supernatural has led to unhelpful distinctions amongst Christian between cultural anthropology and theology. He rejects such a dichotomy, viewing it as an unhelpful approach that is not justified by the biblical writings: he would rather see these two areas of reflection interacting with each other and being unified so that "… a missiologist must become both a Christian anthropologist and a culturally-aware theologian. Anthropology cannot become Christian, nor be truly useful without the merging of these two disciplines."[8]

---

[6] Clifford Geertz, *Interpretation of Cultures: Selected Essays* (New York: Basic Books, 1973), 8.

Tanner, *Theories of Culture,* 31; Kevin Vanhoozer, C. A. Anderson and M.J. Sleasman (eds.) *Everyday Theology: How to Read Cultural Texts and Interpret Trends* (Grand Rapids, MI.: Baker Academic, 2007), 21 & 3.

[7] This concept of worldview is explored more fully in chapter 2.

[8] Gailyn Van Rheenen, "A Theology of Culture: Desecularizing Anthropology," *International Journal of Frontier Missions* 14(1) 1997: 33. Van Rheenen sees this

As he reads the bible, Van Rheenen describes several influences on culture: (1) God is the creator and sustainer of culture; (2) Christ is the transformer of culture; (3) and human beings are God's designated rulers over culture and innovators within culture.[9] There are a number of ramifications for understanding culture as being the subject of God's creation and Christ's cleansing and redemption of culture. God is the God of the nations and both the Old and New Testament attest to God's role amongst the different peoples of the world.[10] Unlike the modern nation-states that we now commonly associate with the term, these "nations" were ethnic groups marked by distinct language and identity. It is *these* nations that Jesus Christ calls us to make disciples of (Matt 28:19), and that we are told will eventually worship him (Rev 7:9; 15:4).

In terms of Jesus Christ's impact on culture, God has sent him into the world at a moment in history to partake of a distinct human culture. Just like Abraham, Moses, and Daniel, Jesus of Nazareth emerged in a particular time, place, and culture, and Christians strive to be loyal to him in their own time, place – and culture. Both Christ Jesus (at a moment in history) and his followers (in the present) were *in* and *of* culture. Jesus Christ's first disciples looked not to a figure who was outside, beyond, or transcendent to culture. Rather, he was a real person whose existence was completely within and a part of their culture. Nevertheless, Jesus was rightly believed by his first disciples to offer enduring wisdom, grace, and hope for all cultures. Their task, therefore, was to discern the meaning of that past cultural event for other cultures. The first disciples engaged in a dialogue with culture. Jesus of Nazareth had not been a figure outside of culture, but a person who spoke within a given culture, offering compelling truth about God's intervention in the world.

There is no 'cultureless' church

This brings us to the second dimension of culture as it connects to the church – the reality that there can be no church that exists as a "cultureless" church. A story is told of kind-hearted baby monkey who, while playing in the trees over a pond, falls in. Upon scrambling out of the water, he notices that there is a fish in the pond. Immediately, he dives back into the water to "rescue" this fish, placing it safely in the tree. Up in the tree, he sees more

---

separation as dating back to the period of the Enlightenment, as ideas about the supernatural started to change with the shift towards rationalism.

[9] Van Rheenen, "A Theology of Culture," 1997, 3-8. Van Rheenen notes that there is a tendency to stress human impact on culture, whilst under-emphasizing the influences of God on culture; he also considers ways in which Satan can be described as a distorter of culture.

[10] Legrand, *The Bible on Culture*, 2000, 132. See: Gen 18:18, Ps 22:27-28, 47:8, 67:2, 96:5-13, Isa 2:1-4, 56:7, 60:3, 66:18, Jer 1:5, Acts 17:26, Rev 15:4, 21:24, and 22:2.

fish. After wedging the thrashing fish in a fork in the tree, he heroically dives back into the pond to rescue the other fish. Just as monkeys are unaware of air – and fish of water – we are unaware of our culture.

Due to our lack of awareness of our culture, we are tempted to think of what we do as somehow being culturally neutral. Nevertheless, like any other building, a church building's design and materials either conspicuously stand out or thoroughly fit into their contexts. In the same way, even among church initiatives that do not simply plant new churches, there is no such thing as a cultureless church. Christian communication, worship, and fellowship, either feels familiar, giving a feeling of being at home, or feels strange. The church-building apprentice, mentioned earlier, could have responded in other ways to his new context. He might have concluded that he would only build churches in places where a level site were possible, importing (perhaps even at considerable expense) foreign building materials in order to build the churches with which he was familiar. Alternatively, he may have built local designs with these foreign materials – or perhaps used local materials to build foreign designs.

The water of life in a cultural cup

To change the analogy, the task of the cross-cultural communicator of Christ can be likened to offering the water of life in a cultural cup. It is simply impossible to drink water out of *nothing*. Something out of which to drink must be chosen – what will it be? An elegant English cup? A trendy ceramic cup? A recyclable plastic, cardboard, or polystyrene mug? A glass? A shaped piece of bamboo? A clay cup? A plastic bag with a straw? While the options are numerous, when offering water to someone, one receptacle must be chosen because everyone drinks out of *something*. A decision to choose one option is a decision *not* to choose any number of others.

Reading the narratives in the book of Acts, as an anthropologist, a number of things strike. Although I am not surprised, I still notice the discrimination of the Hebraic Jews towards those who are Hellenized. Whilst "insiders," in religious terms, those who originated in the Diaspora and spoke Greek were nonetheless perceived in Jerusalem as "outsiders." We realize from this that while religion is an important social marker, so is language, and there are a number of factors that cause people to be viewed as culturally "other." It is reasonable for us to assume that Greek-speaking Jews were the main victims of the persecution and scattering that followed the stoning of Stephen (Acts 7). Despite the fact that these religious refugees were Hellenized Jews, they were still Jews. In the places they were scattered, we are told these Greek speaking Jews shared what God had done in Christ with Jews alone (Acts 11:19). Then, we read the following words (in Acts 11:20-21):

> Some of them, however, men from Cyprus and Cyrene, went to Antioch and began to speak to Greeks also, telling them the good news about the Lord

Jesus. The Lord's hand was with them, and a great number of people believed and turned to the Lord.

This story comes soon after the ground-breaking episode in Acts 10 involving Peter, where the God-fearing Cornelius (a Gentile) heard and believed the news about what God had done in Christ, received the Holy Spirit, and was baptized without becoming a Jew through circumcision. While thoroughly Christian in outlook, Christ's followers in Jerusalem (who had been brought to faith by thoroughly Jewish people) were initially critical of Peter's actions, and were critical of his eventually going up to Jerusalem to explain his actions. We are told, in fact, that the circumcised believers criticized him, saying, "You went into the house of uncircumcised men and ate with them." (Act 11:3). When they eventually heard about what God had done in the name of Jesus, they not only withdrew their objections, but praised God, saying, "So then, even to Gentiles God has granted repentance unto life." (Acts 11: 18) They concluded that God had done a new thing. Although we can only conjecture about the motivation of the Jewish leadership in Jerusalem, dispatching Barnabas to Antioch when they received this news – this is indeed what happened (Acts 11:22).

In Antioch, some years later, we read of Jewish followers of Jesus troubling Gentile followers with statements that becoming a God-fearing convert was inadequate, and with demands that they must become circumcised proselytes (Acts 15:1). As we might imagine, the issue of Gentiles who wanted to become Christians having to follow Jewish cultural norms brought the two groups of the church into sharp dispute. This was the prelude to the Jerusalem council, which is recorded in Acts 15. While some believers insisted that Gentiles must be circumcised and required to obey the Law of Moses, the consensus of the day was that God was doing a new thing. It was decided that there was more than one way of following Jesus: a Jewish way and a Gentile way and that Gentiles did not have to become Jews in order to follow Jesus.

These, and other accounts in Acts, portray the water of life being drunk out of "two cultural cups." Sometimes, Paul is mistakenly misunderstood as giving up his Jewish cultural identity to become a "Christian." Upon his return to Jerusalem, Paul was told, "You see, brother, how many thousands of Jews have believed, and all of them are zealous for the law. They have been informed that you teach all the Jews who live among the Gentiles to turn away from Moses, telling them not to circumcise their children or live according to our customs. (Acts 21:20-21)." As we know, it was only for Gentiles that Paul had strongly discouraged circumcision. James encouraged Paul to prove publicly that he followed Jesus the Messiah, as a Jew, by saying, "Then everyone will know there is no truth in these reports about you, but that you yourself are living in obedience to the law." (Acts 21:24)

Soon after his arrest in the temple, while attempting to clarify his allegiance to the "Jewish cultural cup" (as a follower of Jesus), Paul is accused of being a ringleader of the Nazarene sect (Acts 24:5). In his own defense, Paul clarifies his cultural identity in the following words:

> I admit that I worship the God of our fathers as a follower of the Way, which they call a sect. I believe everything that agrees with the Law and that is written in the Prophets,[15] and I have the same hope in God as these men, that there will be a resurrection of both the righteous and the wicked (Acts 24:14-15).

One of the seminal contributions to mission thinking, by the historian Andrew Walls, has been his highlighting of the difference between conversion and proselytism.[11] Proselytism meant that the "Gentile cup" was entirely discarded and replaced with a Jewish one. Subsequent to the episode involving Cornelius in Acts 10, the innovations in church life from Antioch (recorded in Acts), and the decisions of the Jerusalem council in Act 15, proselytism was replaced with conversion – with the Jerusalem-based (culturally Jewish) disciples and leaders acknowledging that the God of Israel had chosen to fill "Gentile cups" with the Holy Spirit without their becoming Jews first. While the term "proselyte" is rarely heard, proselytism and conversion are synonymous in popular usage.[12] Walls argues that in second temple Judaism, to become a proselyte was to replace one set of beliefs and customs, and to take up those of another people – thus involving the sacrifice of national and social affiliations, constituting a form of naturalization and incorporation into another milieu.[13]

The significance of the Jerusalem Council was the abandonment of the proselyte model in favour of conversion. The main difference between being a convert and a proselyte is that to become a convert is to turn without involving a change of *substance*. Rather, there was a change of *direction*: turning what is already there in a new direction. While proselytism involves "substituting something new for something old, conversion involves redirecting what is already there, turning it in the direction of Christ."[14] Christian conversion in the New Testament did not involve the substitution of one thing for the other, which would constitute moving back to the proselyte model, abandoned by the apostolic church. Furthermore, conversion did not involve adding something new to what is

---

[11] Andrew F. Walls, "Converts for Proselytes? The Crisis over Conversion in the Early Church." *International Bulletin of Missionary Research* 28(1) 2004: 2-7.

[12] Proselytism is commonly conceived as the aggressive proclamation of religious ideas, with people who are successfully proselytized becoming converts.

[13] Interestingly, the proselyte model produced devout Gentile believers who had virtually no impact on their societies. See Andrew F. Walls, "Old Athens and New Jerusalem: some Signposts for Christian Scholarship in the Early History of

already there – supplementing and refining what was already in place. Conversion[15] was less concerned with content than *direction* – turning the whole personality (including its social, cultural, and religious inheritance) toward Christ, thereby opening it up to him.

It is not possible to have a church that is "cultureless." The decision to look one way means you cannot look in another direction. Many things may be drunk out of a cup – even the "living water" that God has given through Christ (John 4). However, it is simply impossible to drink this "living water" out of nothing. An informed decision must be made about both what cultural form is "the cup" from which one drinks, and "the cup" that one offers to others.

Cultures are not "static"

There are few parts of the world unaffected by increased globalization and immigration. As a result of immigration, Asian delights such as *tandoori* chicken and *tom yum* soup can be bought throughout the west; due to globalization, less delightful drinks and fast-foods can also be obtained throughout most of modern-day Asia.

BOOK IDEA

> Jenkins, Philip. *The New Faces of Christianity: Believing the Bible in the Global South.* Oxford: New York: Oxford University Press, 2006.

Cultural settings affect the ways in which people respond to Christianity and how they emphasize different aspects of Christian faith. The author has studied the "global south" and given an insightful survey of ways in which the reception and expression of Christian faith is different from the western world given the different cultural settings and preoccupations. He describes concrete scenarios to give a flavour of 'the new faces of Christianity' but at the same time offers an analysis and critique of this new situation. This book will help readers to think about how culture will shape Christian faith.

Thinking back to our story of the church-builder who has moved to a foreign culture, we can imagine a situation where he could have had other options open to him than purely local materials. He might have arrived at a time when local materials were being superseded by foreign imports. Possibly, foreign materials had begun to be locally manufactured, or there had been increased interest locally in appropriating and adapting foreign influences. Like this shifting and changing choice of building materials, all cultures appear to be subject to "… continuous change, which can sometimes be rapid or sometimes extremely slow. As a result, cultures can

---

[15] Walls, "Converts for Proselytes? 6.

be understood only from a dynamic and diachronic perspective."[16] In other words, we need to recognize the changes that take place in cultures as they respond to external forces and as they change down through the years. Furthermore, there seem to be qualitative differences in the different strengths of the components that make up cultures – it is often the case that an almost unchangeable core exists (often including religious traditions) alongside peripheral and adaptable aspects (illustrated by the way in which cultures are willing to adopt new technologies.)

Walls has described the gospel as both "the prisoner" and "the liberator" of culture: one implication of the incarnation is that whenever Christ has been embraced by people at any time, and in any place, the culture has been sanctified by his presence: Walls refers to this as the "indigenizing principle."[17] He insists that in order for the gospel to penetrate a culture effectively, it must be indigenized and incarnated into that culture. However, not everything in the culture can be "baptized" Christian, and this leads to what Walls terms the "pilgrim principle." This principle is based on the fact that Christians have no abiding city in this world – rather, in order to be faithful to Christ, they must be out of step with their society. Whether in the east or the west, in ancient time or modern, no society has ever existed that absorbed the word of Christ painlessly into its system.[18]

Further Reading on Culture and Ministry

Carter, C. A. *Rethinking Christ and Culture: A Post-Christendom Perspective.* Grand Rapids: Brazos Press, 2006.

Gorringe, T. J. *Furthering Humanity: a Theology of Culture.* Aldershot: Ashgate, 2004.

Jenkins, P. *The Next Christendom: The Coming of Global Christianity.* (Rev. ed.) Oxford: Oxford University Press, 2007.

Vanhoozer, K. (ed.) *Everyday Theology. How to Read Cultural Trends and Interpret Texts.* Grand Rapids, MI: Baker, 2010.

Walls, A. F. *Missionary Movement in Christian History: Studies in the Transmission of Faith.* Maryknoll: Orbis, 1996.

---

[16] E. Nunnenmacher, "Culture," in *Dictionary of Mission: Theology, History, Perspectives,* ed. by K. Müller et al, 94-8 (Maryknoll, N.Y.: Orbis Books, 1997), 95.

[17] Andrew F. Walls, "The Gospel as the Prisoner and Liberator of Culture," *Missionalia* 10(3) 1982:97-98.

[18] Walls, "The Gospel as the Prisoner and Liberator of Culture," 182, 99; see also C. Geffre,"Christianity and Culture," *International Review of Mission* 84 (332/333) 1995:17-31. Claude Geffre make similar observations, commenting that as well as Christianity being indigenized, cultures are also Christianized.

Conclusion

It remains a real challenge to make the gospel culturally intelligible and to help local people to assimilate it in every context where it is preached. Sharing the gospel meaningfully requires that the gospel is not only "translated into the languages and culture of local people" but that it is done in a way that "must sustain them for the long haul." This is partly the role of the church, in making visible the gospel in the lives of Christians within any given culture. Although facilitating the reception of the gospel constitutes a challenge in any culture, it should never be unintelligible, nor should the form of the gospel be seen as being at odds with the local culture.

"If we believe that grace builds on nature, we can then forge theological and missiological links with anthropology."[19] More than any other of the social sciences, anthropology helps cross-cultural ambassadors to interpret the local, and facilitate a translation of the gospel so that they can share what God has done in Christ, creatively and contextually. In order for Christ's ambassadors to present a clear message, they must be equally conversant with both the Word of God and the world in which they are living. Our ability to read local cultures needs to be as sophisticated as our ability to read scriptural texts. Indeed, Kevin Vanhoozer argues for cultural competency so that Christian communicators can "read, exegete, and expound" cultures as competently as they can do these things in relation to the biblical text.[20]

We have suggested that culture was created by God and redeemed by Christ, who commissions his followers and ambassadors to transform cultures in their turn. Culture is a good gift from God, but cultures are not static, and to become a culture-watcher is a vital part of becoming an effective communicator of the gospel. There are two reasons for this: firstly, as we become aware of our cultures, we are better equipped to see how they shape our own understanding of the gospel; secondly, we will be able to communicate the gospel more effectively both within our own culture and cross-culturally. We have also seen that there can be no church which is a "cultureless" church and that it is not possible to drink water "out of nothing" – there needs to be a culturally appropriate "cup" from which to drink. The story of the first cross-culture communicators, as recorded in the book of Acts, is that of people who offer "the water of life" to Gentiles in their own cups. This is "the indigenizing principle" that forms the first chapter of a story that shows how God, through God's cross-cultural ambassadors, and with the activity of the Holy Spirit, will transform each and every culture.

---

[19] Anthony. J. Gittins, "Anthropology," in *Dictionary of Mission: Theology, History, Perspectives* ed. by K. Müller et al (Maryknoll, N.Y.: Orbis Books, 1997), 27.
[20] Vanhoozer, *Everyday Theology,* 2007.

Questions for Reflection/ Discussion

1. Why does the author use the metaphor of a cup from which to drink? What point is he trying to make about contextualization?
2. How does the author (following Walls) differentiate "proselytism" and "conversion"? Why is it significant that "conversion is about a change of direction?
3. "Our ability to read local cultures needs to be as sophisticated as our ability to read scriptural texts." Think about one culture that you know which is different from your own. Give two or three examples of how people act in a way which reflects a particular cultural value: support your examples with evidence from real-life or from stories associated with the culture.

WORLDVIEW AND CONTEXTUALIZATION

Phil Nicholson

Phil Nicholson shows how ministry can be enhanced with a deeper understanding of worldview, by reflecting on current thinking about worldviews and relating this to his ministry experience in Taiwan. He explores the nature of worldview and points out a number of practical ways in which the cross-cultural worker can find out what people's beliefs and behaviours really are. He concludes with thoughts on how an understanding of worldview can help those in ministry transform other people's lives and he shares examples of contextualized ministry relating to groups in Taiwan who hold worldviews shaped by animism.

When I first arrived in Taiwan, in the early 1990s, I came with the intention of working with university students. After studying Mandarin for two years, I started ministry in the capital city of Taipei and, like many missionaries, proceeded to use methods and tools that I was familiar with from my home country of Australia. I am thankful that the students with whom I worked were gracious to a foreigner who had a limited understanding of the world in which they lived: their level of education and understanding of Western culture allowed them to "interpret" my words and actions. As I interacted more with colleagues who primarily worked with working class or marginalised groups of people (who had more modest education), I realised that they faced an even greater cultural gap and often served among people who simply did not understand the message that they were presenting. I think that I had been living in Taiwan for about ten years, before I began to understand what most Taiwanese people really believe and value.

My problems were two-fold: firstly, as Taiwan is an advanced and developed society, my initial response had been to see the external, wealthy, modern façade and assume that Taiwanese people were just the same as I was (with my Western cultural background.) I made little allowance for any significant differences in the way that I sought to present the gospel or teach God's word. Over time, I modified my methods of communicating, through trial and error, but without really understanding why this was necessary. Secondly, I discovered that most people identified themselves as Buddhist or Taoist and I made an effort to better understand these religions. However, neither of these formal religions seemed to really make sense of Taiwanese culture and religious practice. People would claim to be Buddhist but not act in the way that my seminary training had taught me Buddhists should behave. A breakthrough occurred when it was shown to me that most Taiwanese people are neither western nor Buddhist but rather animistic. All that I had been observing finally started to make sense. It has only been in clearly identifying the *worldview* of the people amongst whom I work that it has been possible for me to present effectively the gospel in a way that speaks to their hearts, challenging, confronting and comforting them so that they are willing to place their faith in Jesus Christ.

A person's worldview is what lies at the heart of their belief system and culture. Although, by the grace of God, we can be used in ministry while remaining ignorant of people's worldview, we will be much more effective if we are able to understand and speak to a person's worldview. Whether we engage in evangelism or discipleship training, our goal in ministry is to see people transformed by the gospel at the deepest level of their lives. This includes having their worldview challenged and reshaped. The danger we face if we do not take into account worldview is that we will end up having to be content with superficial change that is neither lasting nor substantial.[1] Therefore, understanding a person's worldview is of crucial importance if we are to communicate effectively. It is a prerequisite for contextualization – the effective and relevant communication of the gospel. Contextualization is built upon a prior understanding of worldview. This chapter will consider what we mean by worldview, it will offer some simple methods that we can use to identify the worldview of the people with whom we minister, and it will consider the relationship between worldview and contextualization.

The Nature of Worldview

The term "worldview" is used with a number of different meanings so it is important to define what is being referred to in this chapter. Sometimes worldview is used to refer to a coherent belief system that answers life's metaphysical questions, and we could talk, for example, about a Christian worldview based on a biblical theology. This could be compared with competing worldviews such as atheism, naturalism, Buddhism, and so on. Such an approach is often used in apologetics where the relative values of different worldviews are argued.[2] However, the concern here is not an ideological worldview but rather the actual beliefs and lived out worldview of the people with whom we minister. There may be significant departures from the worldview which they *claim* to hold: examples would be the professed atheist who still takes note of the daily horoscope; the Buddhist who wears an amulet for protection; or the Christian who seeks medical help when sick but neglects to pray. In each of these cases, their behaviour

---

[1] Paul Hiebert, "Conversion and Worldview Transformation," *International Journal of Frontier Missions* 14 (2) 1997: 83-86.

[2] See for example Graham Cole, "Do Christians have a worldview?" The Gospel Coalition. http://www.thegospelcoalition.org/pdf-articles/Cole.pdf (accessed 22nd May 2012). Cole suggests that a worldview must be both "thinkable" (consistently helps us make sense of the world) and "livable" (corresponds to experience) in order to be of value.

says something about their worldview which is at odds with their stated belief system. Let's imagine the following dialogue:

"What do you believe?"

A Christian may answer, "I believe I believe in God the Father, Almighty, Maker of heaven and earth: and in Jesus Christ, his only begotten Son..."

"No, what do you *really* believe?!"

It is not hard to answer the first question. We learn what we should believe and with some practice we can recite it in the form of a creed or a list of statements. "What do you *really* believe?" is a totally different question. It is not merely a matter of what we verbally agree to, but what actually determines our actions, our values, and our entire way of life. What is it that determines how we raise our children and relate to our spouse? What is it that really affects the way we handle our money, the way we respond to a crisis or the way that we use our time? When we find the answers to these and to similar questions about what we really believe, then we begin to describe our worldview.

Questions to help analyze worldview

Worldview is such a broad concept that it is sometimes hard to know what is actually meant by it. A simple, but helpful analysis, is to regard a worldview as answering fundamental questions about life. For example, Walsh and Middleton[3] say that worldviews answer four ultimate question about life:

Who am I? – what is the nature, task and significance of human beings?

Where am I? – what is the origin and nature of the reality in which human beings find themselves?

What's wrong? – how can we account for the distortion and brokenness in this reality?

What's the remedy? – how can we alleviate this brokenness, if at all?

To this list, others would add questions such as: "how do we know?" (epistemology); "what is time and history?"; and "what is good?" (ethics). Answering these types of questions will not necessarily provide a comprehensive perspective on worldview, but it will at least provide a broader framework of understanding. We will explore below how to begin answering these and other more specific questions that can lead us towards understanding another person's worldview.

---

[3] Brian Walsh and Richard Middleton, *The Transforming Vision: Shaping a Christian Worldview* (Downers Grove, IL: Inter Varsity Press, 1984).

The Onion model of culture

A simple way of understanding worldview is to use the "onion model" of culture.[4] As we explore the culture of an individual or a people group, what we first see is *behaviour*: the things that people do. (This includes both individual actions and the wide variety of customs and traditions found in a culture.) Behaviour can be explained by the different *values* that people have, by what they think is important or right or good. Values in turn grow out of people's *beliefs*: beliefs about the world, about themselves, and about God. Finally, at the deepest level we find *worldview*: this is our picture of reality, the "story" that we believe about why the world is the way it is. Such an analysis raises the question of why it is that worldview holds such a central place. What is it about worldview that gives it such importance?

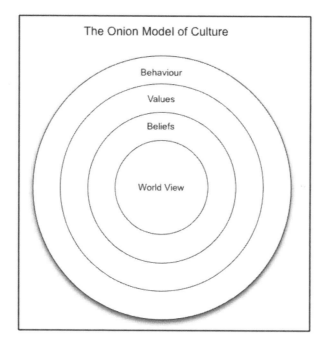

The Onion Model of Culture

Behaviour

Values

Beliefs

World View

---

[4] I first came across this model at seminary; there seem to be a number of versions. It has been suggested that Eugene Bunkowske, Ph.D., developed the "Cultural Onion Diagram" during his early years as Graduate Professor of Biblical Missiology at Concordia Theological Seminary. See http://resources. campusforchrist.org/index.php/Onion_diagram (accessed 22nd May 2012).

A Definition of Worldview

The Willowbank Report describes worldview as simply "a general understanding of the nature of the universe and of one's place in it."[5] Similarly, the American Heritage Dictionary defines it as "a collection of beliefs about life and the universe held by an individual or a group." However, it is more than just the sum of our beliefs. On the one hand, our observable culture expresses our worldview. Our beliefs and actions reveal our explicit and implicit assumptions about the world and ourselves. On the other hand, worldview acts to interpret our experiences. It is a paradigm which controls what we accept and what we reject. As a result, worldview has been variously and helpfully described as an "overall perspective," a "frame of reference,"[6] or "a way of seeing the world."[7] A worldview is like a pair of glasses which brings into focus all our different experiences of life. Here is a useful definition, which fits with the ideas found in this chapter:

> A worldview is a set of presuppositions (assumptions which may be true, partially true or entirely false) which we hold (consciously or subconsciously, consistently or inconsistently) about the basic make-up of our world.[8]

A number of features of this definition should be noted. Firstly, a worldview is not just a list of beliefs but includes the presuppositions that lie *behind* our beliefs. These presuppositions can act as a "touchstone"[9] by which we evaluate other ideas and experiences. For example, naturalism denies the existence of any supernatural reality. This is a "touchstone" which rules out the possibility of the occurrence of miracles or of any other supernatural phenomenon. Any argument which relies on the existence of a supernatural realm is dismissed out of hand because it is refuted by the presuppositions. This means that worldviews, though inherently subjective, are seen to be rational by those who hold them.

Taiwanese people and their beliefs

Taiwanese people believe strongly in fate, fortune telling, protective charms and the efficacy of occult activities. They are often described as very superstitious by western observers. The implication is that they are

---

[5] Lausanne Committee on World Evangelization, Lausanne Occasional Paper 2: "The Willowbank Report – Consultation on Gospel and Culture, 1978," http://www.lausanne.org/en/documents/lops/73-lop-2.html (accessed 22nd May 2012).

[6] Cole, "Do Christians have a worldview?"

[7] David Hesselgrave, *Communicating Christ Cross-Culturally* (2nd ed.) (Grand Rapids, MI: Zondervan, 1991), 161 ff.

[8] James Sire, *The Universe Next Door* (Downers Grove, IL: Inter Varsity Press, 1988), 17.

[9] Cole, "Do Christians have a worldview?" 3.

foolish and gullible, open to believe anything. Western people, including Christian workers, have a tendency to dismiss the reality of these spiritual forces through the use of reason. However, the occult practices and beliefs within Taiwan's folk religions make sense from the perspective of their animistic worldview. Taiwanese people can point to apparently supernatural experiences which they interpret to confirm the reality of what they believe. There is an internal logic that outsiders, with different presuppositions, can easily miss and dismiss. Their religious practices reflect a worldview and are not just uncontrolled or foolish superstition.

The second aspect of the definition to note is that worldviews can be true or false. Any functional worldview will have some internal consistency.[10] This does not mean that it necessarily provides a true reflection of reality. However, we often remain committed to our worldviews, even when they are in error, because they seem to help us to make sense of our world, provide answers in times of crisis, and help to bind a community together. There is a large, personal and perhaps social cost in changing worldviews. "People are… reluctant to change their worldview unless it proves totally inadequate to help them cope with their current situation."[11] Therefore, pointing out the disconnection between a person's worldview and their experience of the world may have little impact, since holding a worldview is not a purely objective or rational matter. Thirdly, the definition notes that worldviews can be held "consciously or subconsciously, consistently or inconsistently…" This is important because when we consider contextualization, what concerns us is not an idealized or theoretical worldview, but rather that which is actually held by the people we are addressing. They will have a worldview (a series of presuppositions by which they live), but they may not always be aware consciously of what these are. Moreover, there may be inconsistencies and contradictions in what they believe. Many Christians working in other cultures have found themselves in the position of teaching professed Buddhists what they *should* believe as Buddhists, in order then to challenge this *idealized* Buddhist worldview. It is probably more fruitful, in such circumstances to recognize that there will be a difference between what people *should* believe (in terms of their stated worldview) and what they actually *do* believe, and to be ready to interact with them "as they are."

Suggested Reading on Worldview

Burnett, David. *Clash of Worlds.* Crowborough: MARC, 1990.

---

[10] One definition suggests "A worldview consists of basic assumptions and images that provide a more or less coherent, though not necessarily accurate, way of thinking about the world." See Mynga Futrell, "Worldview Diversity," Teaching about Religion: in Support of Civic Pluralism, http://www.teachingaboutreligion. org/worldviewdiversity.html (accessed 22nd May 2012)

[11] David Burnett, *Clash of Worlds* (Crowborough: MARC, 1990), 21-22.

Goheen, Michael W. and Craig G. Bartholomew. *Living at the Crossroads: an Introduction to Christian Worldview.* Grand Rapids, MI: Baker Academic, 2008.
Naugle, David K. *Worldview: The History of a Concept.* Grand Rapids, MI: Eerdmans, 2002.
Philip Graham Ryken and David S. Dockery. *Christian Worldview: a Student's Guide.* Wheaton, IL: Crossway, 2013. (Reclaiming the Christian Intellectual Tradition.)

Exploring Worldview

For Christian communicators, the basic reason for seeking to understand a person's worldview is to know how to present the gospel in such a way that it makes sense in light of their worldview. This is what is meant by the concept of contextualization and it is a necessary activity at every stage of Christian ministry. The aim of contextualization is not to make the gospel easier to accept, but rather to ensure it is correctly understood and relevantly applied. In contextualizing we seek to understand a worldview and to identify both barriers to the gospel and also possible bridges or contact points that will help us to communicate clearly. A second reason why it is important to take time identifying the worldviews of other people is that this helps us to see more clearly our own worldview.

> Worldviews are largely implicit...worldviews are the glasses through which people look, not what the people look at. Often we become aware of our own worldview only when we live deeply in another culture, and then return to our own culture through outside eyes, with a different belief and value system.[12]

Identifying the worldview of others helps us to be more aware of our own worldview and the ways it influences our presentation and practice of the gospel. So our first task is to discover the worldview of the people we are working amongst. Finding a worldview is easier said than done. You can ask a person: "What do you do in such and such a situation?" You can ask: "What do you believe?" and you may get a clear answer. However, you cannot simply ask: "What is your worldview?" The problem is not simply that this is a strange question. Most people are not aware of what their worldview is and are simply not able to articulate how they view reality in any systematic way. Even if you were to get an answer to this question there is no guarantee it would be accurate. This is because your worldview is not what you *say* you believe, but what you *really* believe!

Reflecting on worldview

Sometimes it is difficult to know where to begin. Here are a few suggestions about how we can start to get under the surface of a culture, to

---

[12] Hiebert, "Conversion and Worldview Transformation," *IJFM*, 85.

make sense of the often confusing and, to our eyes, strange customs of other peoples. There are several ways in which we can reflect on worldview. Firstly, we can work at understanding the biblical dimensions of our own worldview ensuring that it is built on a good biblical foundation. In seeking to reach animistic people we have found it tremendously helpful to make use of the method which seeks to communicate the gospel by telling the big story of the Bible in oral story form.[13] Many Christians who have started using this approach have been surprised to find how this has informed their own biblical worldview and have realized that much of their previous Christian understanding was piecemeal and only sufficient to answer a narrow set of (often personal) questions. Their understanding fell short of being an overall perspective sufficient to address the many different challenges faced in applying the gospel in a complex world. A fully biblical worldview will give us a foundation by which we can interpret and critique other worldviews. A biblical worldview comes primarily through being biblically literate and especially through understanding the overall storyline or meta-narrative of the scriptures. However, it is also helpful to take time to read other material which presents the teaching of the Bible in terms of worldview questions. Secondly, we can become familiar with some of the cultural or social theories that give us tools which we can use to study a worldview. Although there are a great number of different worldviews, these can be broken down into a smaller number of categories using diagnostic tools developed by researchers.

Mary Douglas's grid-group theory classifies social groups according to two variables, termed "group" (which has to do with social integration) and "grid" (which has to do with social constraint).[14] This cultural theory leads to identifying four basic worldviews: 1) individualism (weak group, weak grid); 2) hierarchism (strong group, strong grid); 3) fatalism (weak group, strong grid); and 4) egalitarianism (strong group, weak grid). Traditional Chinese culture with its Confucian influenced family and social structures would be classified as hierarchism. It is a group-oriented society in which almost all relationships are hierarchically arranged. The relevance of this is that "how people relate to one another in a social group gives some important clues on their worldviews and values."[15] So for example, in Chinese culture the authority of a statement depends largely on the status of the person who makes it. By observing how people interact socially, we can gain insight into their worldview.

Lingenfelter and Mayers use a model based on contrasting pairs of values. They present six contrasting pairs of basic values which vary from

---

[13] Christine Dillon, *Telling the Gospel through Story: Evangelism that Keeps Hearers Wanting More* (Leicester: IVP, 2012).

[14] Mary Douglas, *Natural Symbols: Explorations in Cosmology* (London: Barrie and Rockcliff, 1970).

[15] Dr Nick Meader, private correspondence, April 2008.

culture to culture: a) "time orientation" versus "event orientation"; b) "task orientation" versus "person orientation"; c) "dichotomistic thinking" versus "holistic thinking"; d) "status focus" versus "achievement focus"; e) "crisis orientation" versus "non-crisis orientation"; f) "concealment of vulnerability" versus "willingness to expose vulnerability."[16] These contrasting pairs of values are a tool designed to assist in cross-cultural relationships. However, using this type of framework to analyze a target culture can also provide information about worldview and can help to explain behaviour and beliefs.

For example, a western doctor is frustrated with his Taiwanese nurses because they report to him that they have no more life-saving pills, only when the last bottle is empty. They did not place an order for more pills two weeks previously when the last bottle was half empty. When the doctor understands that Taiwanese culture has a non-crisis orientation he is better able to understand this behaviour and develop a strategy to manage the situation. At the same time the doctor gains a valuable insight into the worldview which lies behind this behaviour. Finally, there has been a significant amount of research into many of the cultures of Asia – those in ministry should make time to read social and anthropological research that can be an invaluable resource for understanding worldview. There are a number of books which introduce the concept of worldview in more depth and provide a comparison of how common worldviews (including the biblical worldview) answer key worldview questions. Such material can provide an overall framework by which to analyse any specific worldview.

Questionnaire to help discern worldviews

For those engaged in ministry, there is a need to go beyond reading the research and observations of others. General reading can give us the broad strokes of a culture and its underlying worldview. However, worldviews vary with time and place. It is essential we do not assume the people we meet adhere to a "textbook version" of a worldview but take time to observe and question the actual people amongst whom we work. We can learn much about a person's worldview by seeking answers to questions, whether general questions (such as the four ultimate questions listed above), or whether more specific cultural questions. Burnett suggests asking the following ten questions:[17]

What beliefs are strongly held?

How do parents teach children to behave?

What do people regard as major offences (sins)?

---

[16] Sherwood G. Lingenfelter and M. K. Mayers, *Ministering Cross-Culturally: An Incarnational Model for Personal Relationships.* (Grand Rapids, MI: Baker, 1986.)
[17] See David Burnett, *Clash of Worlds* p. 26-29 for a more detailed explanation of each of these questions.

What do people do in crisis?

What rituals do people perform?

Who are the trend-setters?

What are the greatest fears people have?

What are considered to be words of wisdom?

What is expressed in the art forms of the people?

What aspects of the culture are most resistant to change?

There are also a number of comprehensive cultural questionnaires available which can help provide an even more detailed analysis.[18] The purpose of such a list of questions is to alert us to the many areas in which cultures can differ. We can use this questionnaire directly by asking people for answers to the questions. Alternatively, the questions can function to help us be more aware and observant of a culture and thinking about the worldview that lies at its heart.

Observation activity

Apart from directly asking questions we can train ourselves to observe and analyse what we see in another culture. If a worldview lies behind behaviour, values and beliefs, then we need to start understanding a worldview by simply observing these things that we can actually see. For example, we can pursue the following questions:

Worldview Activity

Observation: *(Record what you see; anything interesting, unusual, surprising, thought-provoking.)*

Reflection: *(How did this make me feel? Why? What does this tell me about myself and my beliefs?)*

Explanation: *(Why did this occur? What does it mean? What does this tell me about the values and beliefs of the people?)*

The explanation step can be carried out in discussion with others, by asking local people or by doing further research. As this activity depends on our own responses, it particularly draws attention to areas where the worldview of the people differs from our own. It has the additional benefit of helping us to be more aware of our own values, beliefs and prejudices.

---

[18] One example can be found online on the Oral Strategies site. See "Constructing a worldview," Orality Strategies, http://www.oralitystrategies.org/resources.cfm?id =550&Search=worldview (accessed 22nd May 2012).

This activity works best when we are new to a culture and more sensitive to the differences from home. This simple activity can help us to be more sensitive to and reflective of what takes place around us.

Ministry issues

As worldview is all encompassing it may be helpful to focus more narrowly on the areas which impact more directly on our ministry. For example, we can ask the following types of questions:

Evangelism – What are the barriers to the gospel? What are the bridges to the gospel?

Discipleship – What are the barriers to the Christian maturity? What does a godly believer look like in this culture?

Church planting – In this culture, what does a Christian community look like? What are appropriate times and places to meet? How will godly leadership be expressed?

(These and similar questions will be taken up in more detail in the chapters that follow.)

BOOK IDEA

Hiebert, Paul. *Transforming Worldviews: an Anthropological Understanding of how People Change*. Grand Rapids, MI: Baker Academic, 2008.

This book offers advice on understanding and analyzing worldviews. It looks at a range of modern categorizations of worldview for different cultural settings. It shows that Christian faith involves more than a choice to share in certain rituals and activities. It outlines a biblical worldview, showing the importance of putting Jesus Christ at the centre of life and the impact that this has on outlook and behaviour leading to "transformation." The book makes clear the link between a deep understanding of cultures and the transformation of worldview.

Worldview and the Taiwanese Context

In what follows, I would like to show how this kind of thinking applies to my own ministry context in Taiwan. Currently, our organisation is focused on "working class communities" who are strongly animistic and have not been effectively reached with the gospel.

The character of folk religion in Taiwan

Religious rituals are extremely important in Taiwanese folk religion. Public processions are common: these include dressing up as religious figures, music, dance, fireworks, religious offerings and often a common meal; they are noisy, colourful, and fun. These not only have significant religious meaning, bringing fortune and protection to worshippers, they are lively community activities. Young men in particular enjoy participating. This kind of religion can be seen, heard, smelled and touched. Modern Christianity tends to focus on "the word" and eschews religious rituals. The challenge we face in Taiwan is to show that the gospel is not abstract or ethereal, only dealing with distant eternal issues. If we minister to such people as if they are modernists or strict Buddhists, we will fail to show that the gospel is also concrete and relevant to the immediate needs of the individual and the community. This means seeking to introduce appropriate public activities, objects and pictures that point to the truth and draw a connection between it and their felt needs of protection from spiritual forces, health problems, financial concerns and a sense of belonging.

Some of the methods we have adopted to express this, are as follows: using pictures illustrating key Bible stories to decorate ministry centres; engaging in prayer ceremonies which ask for protection on ministry buildings and the homes of believers; holding activities in public spaces such as parks and on the street rather than behind closed doors (whenever possible); acting out Bible stories corporately; eating together regularly, both after Sunday worship and on special days such as the Mid-Autumn Festival. The purpose of these activities is to show that the gospel is concrete, interesting, and relevant to individuals and the community. These approaches happen alongside, not in place of, preaching and explaining the gospel orally.

Taiwan's working class people also have a strong awareness of the supernatural and so in times of crisis or difficulty will seek supernatural solutions. Traditionally, this involves temple offerings, visiting fortune-tellers and the use of amulets, charms and the like. Rather than using rational or theological explanations to deny the effectiveness of such efforts, this is an ideal situation to show the relevance of the gospel. By immediately praying with and for people in times of crisis we show our faith in the power and care of our God. And as they see such prayers answered they also start to consider the alternatives offered by the gospel. Whereas naturalistic Westerners may seek to explain away answered prayers as coincidence or wishful thinking, those coming from an animistic worldview do not question the reality of supernatural solutions to everyday problems.

Worldview and Contextualization

Our goal in ministry is not just to influence people's behaviour: we need to go beyond changing behaviour to changing underlying beliefs, otherwise people will just be conforming externally to the gospel. We need to strive to go even deeper and help people to realign their worldview in accordance with the Scriptures. If the gospel only brings change at the level of beliefs, the result will be a shallow, inconsistent and syncretistic faith.

When we are serving amongst people with a different culture, paying attention to worldview is both more important and more difficult. They 'see' the world differently from ourselves and the words we speak may not be heard the way we intend. Miscommunication may be on the level of misunderstanding the words we use. A recent advertising campaign is a good illustration of this: the campaign promotes the company *HSBC* as "The world's local bank." It emphasizes the importance of local knowledge and cultural understanding. For example, one poster shows three pictures all labelled "cutlery." Each picture shows a hand, the first holding a pair of chopsticks is labelled "Singapore"; the second, labelled "United Kingdom," shows a knife and fork; and the third, picturing fingers, "India." Miscommunication is very easy if we do not have agreed understanding of the actions, ideas and words we are using. Even words that we may think are clear, such as "God", "sin", "forgiveness", "love", also all take on very different meanings in different cultures with different worldviews.

A failure to consider the worldview of our listeners can also mean that we are simply not heard at all. We may find ourselves answering questions that people are not asking, addressing non-issues and failing to consider matters of vital importance. Within my ministry context in Taiwan, the danger faced by Christians from outside the culture, is to overlook the animistic worldview held by most people. It is often assumed that people are either Buddhist or Taoist or a combination of these. However, it is more accurate to describe these religions as the outward structures by which people to express their animistic beliefs. There is a core of animism wrapped in the clothes of Chinese religious beliefs – even if a person identifies themselves as a Buddhist, there is little value trying to argue about Buddhist philosophy if, in their heart, they are an animist.

A further complication is that the typical foreign Christian, with a university education, seeks to communicate the gospel out of a worldview that may be heavily influenced by secular Western values. The result is that animistic people, whose lives are concerned with daily issues of power, and peace, are confronted with preaching that emphasizes ultimate questions of truth and forgiveness of sin. The result is that the gospel is seen as foreign and irrelevant, or else there is a positive response, but only on a superficial level. Animistic folk religion is concerned with making use of the powers of supernatural forces and beings for personal benefit. The promises of the gospel of Jesus Christ are very easily seen as another means of doing this same thing. Jesus is incorporated into their pantheon of gods to whom prayers can be offered.

Animism is a human-centred religion that operates on a principle of mutual benefit to the worshippers and those worshipped. When gods fail to respond to prayers, worshippers may choose to abandon a god who fails them and try another. If the gospel is accepted by a person who retains an animistic worldview, when Jesus fails to answer prayers positively, they may either abandon their faith or else may assume that this request is outside of Jesus' area of authority and seek help from another source. In this situation, it is clear that any communication of the gospel needs to address the question of the spiritual powers that are sought by animists. When explaining the gospel, it is helpful to begin with stories such as the description of the creation and the fall of human beings, in the book of Genesis, in order to establish the nature of God and his relationship to both the natural and supernatural realms. This can lead to an understanding of the character of Jesus as the Son of God who is radically different from other spiritual beings and who has a unique power and authority. The animistic worldview of the people with whom we talk does not limit or control our presentation of the gospel. However, unless the gospel is presented in a way that penetrates the fundamental level of people's animistic beliefs and assumptions their faith will be superficial and fragile.

We see a number of examples of this within the scriptures. When the prophets caustically ridicule those who worship idols, they are generally addressing God's people[19] and their attacks are not designed as an evangelistic strategy to the nations but rather seek to undermine Israel's temptation to idolatry by exposing the futility of a worldview that sees value in idol worship. In fact, much of the Old Testament is taken up with establishing a worldview with Yahweh as Creator and Redeemer as against the animistic worldviews of the surrounding nations. In the New Testament, John the Baptist criticises the Pharisees, not just regarding their behaviour, but also concerning their assumptions regarding election.[20] In their worldview, their heritage as Abraham's descendants has become a badge of honour and an excuse to sin rather than a cause of thankful obedience. Their basic assumptions need to be challenged. Jesus likewise challenges the Sadducees' assumptions that deny the possibility of resurrection.[21] Paul, in speaking to the polytheistic Athenians, masterfully both appeals to and undermines their view of reality.[22] In each of these cases, the speakers not only challenge the surface issues of religion or morality, but also have an understanding of the presuppositions of the listeners and take care to address these. It is therefore of vital importance that we take time to look beyond the behaviour and stated values and beliefs of the people we work amongst, to seek to understand the

---

[19] See for example Jer 10.

[20] Matt 3:9.

[21] Matt 22:29-32.

[22] Acts 17:24-31. D. Carson says only "after he has set out an entire worldview, and even something of a philosophy of history, does Paul introduce Jesus." He goes on to claim that "the good news of Jesus Christ is virtually incoherent unless it is securely set into a biblical worldview" Don Carson, *The Gagging of God* (Grand Rapids, MI: Zondervan, 1996), 50-52.

worldview which drives these. Only then can we consider how to challenge this worldview with the gospel, whether in evangelism or discipleship.

Conclusion

An understanding of worldview lays a foundation for effective and biblically faithful contextualization. Such an understanding must include both the worldview of the Bible and that of the people amongst whom we work. Without this understanding, contextualization faces a number of dangers: it can become trivial, dealing with only the external issues of dress, food and other customs; or it can slip easily into accommodation with the target culture and possible syncretism. In the attempt to be contextual, we can adopt local patterns of behaviour, failing to see they are reflective of a worldview that is in conflict with biblical truth. Alternatively, overlooking worldview may lead us to be blind to the impact of our own culture on our values and practices. In this instance, our ministry may be more driven by our own cultural background than by the scriptures and, as a result, the model of Christian faith and practice that we communicate will be inappropriate in our target culture. If we are to be effective communicators of the gospel, we must spend time understanding the worldview that lies beneath the surface of a culture, and consider how this will affect the way we communicate the gospel in each and every aspect of our ministry.

Questions For Reflection/Discussion

1. The author considers the importance of a "biblical worldview": have you given sufficient thought to the meta-narrative (the overarching story) of the bible. Summarize it in a few sentences; consider how it shapes your thinking about life. Are there ways in which you might need to think further about the "biblical worldview" and its implications?
2. Sketch out responses to Burnett's questions about culture and worldview for a culture that you know well. As a result of this activity; respond to the following two questions: Are there gaps in your thinking or knowledge of this culture? What insights do they give you about this culture?
3. "If we are to be effective communicators of the gospel, we must spend time understanding the worldview that lies beneath the surface of a culture… "What are some of the issues that lie "beneath the surface" of a culture that interests you?

PART TWO

REFLECTIONS ON MINISTRY

CONTEXTUALIZATION AND EVANGELISM

Daniel D. Kim

Daniel Kim shows that the methods and content of evangelism need to take account of culture. Christians who cross cultures need to be ready to adapt and change their approaches in new contexts: those who engage in short-term mission need to be especially careful in this regard. The author looks back to the New Testament for inspiration and then he considers practical ways in which people who share the gospel need to take account of their identity as a messenger, their lifestyle and their hearers' reactions to the concepts they are sharing. He concludes with thoughts on the role of "community" and of "prayer" in relation to evangelism.

Contextualization has become one of the most discussed topics in mission since the 1970s. With a growing awareness of the recent developments in contextualization, Christians in Asia have begun to adopt contextualized approaches to evangelism rather than simply using forms of evangelism that are adapted from foreign models. Asian Christians are increasingly aware that unless the gospel of Jesus Christ is presented in the contexts of Asia in ways that connect with local people's language, culture, and world view, Christian efforts at evangelization will be prone to failure.

As an Asian who has spent periods of time living both in Asia and in the west, I would like to explore this theme of evangelism and its relationship to contextualization more carefully. At present, I work with the church in northern Thailand and teach as a lecturer in theology at Chiang Mai Theological Seminary. As part of my work, I interact with church leaders from around Thailand and I have often asked them this question: "What do you see as the greatest need for the churches in Thailand today?" Since the percentage of Thai Christians is very small, I had expected them to stress the need for more evangelism. However, to my surprise, the majority of them expressed real misgivings about the Thai church's inability to nurture active and mature disciples *after* people have embraced Christian faith. In other words, Thai churches seem to engage in evangelism that is not really effective: approaches to evangelism that are not adequately contextualized do not lead to Christians whose lives are transformed into genuine expressions of Christian faith in the Thai context.

Contextualization and Evangelism

Those who live in the west are becoming more aware that evangelism is shaped by context. In a recent book on evangelism, Michael Green spells out the great changes in the cultural climate that have taken place during the last twenty-five years. These changes have critical implications for the church and it cannot simply adopt traditional methods of evangelism but instead needs to contextualize its methods of evangelism to be relevant to the current generation.[1] Unlike the "modern" outlook, the "postmodern" worldview tends to reject notions of "absolute truth" and those who choose a postmodern outlook cannot easily be reached by declarations about faith alone. As a result, Dean Flemming wisely suggests that there are three essential components involved in presenting the gospel in a postmodern world: these are story, imagination and a community which models the gospel and to which people can belong.[2] In short, we now recognize that in western contexts, we must adjust our methods of evangelism if we are to reach the postmodern generation and people from different cultural backgrounds.

Evangelism and context in western and non-western worlds

In the same way, we need to make comparable adjustments if we engage in evangelism with people in non-western contexts like Asia. Many Asian people will be completely unaware of the message of the Christian scriptures and will have no knowledge of Christian stories, imagery or ideas. How effective would our evangelism be to Buddhists in a country like Thailand if we adopted either a traditional western or a postmodern approach to evangelism? As Christians who seek to share the gospel and evangelize in Asia, we need to play down or minimize the cultural representation of Jesus that is shaped by western culture, and instead emphasize and underline the cultural representations of Jesus that fit with Thai culture.

One advocate of contextualized evangelism is Tom Steffen, who seeks to promote culturally appropriate evangelism and as a consequence rejects methods of evangelism that are simply transferred from the west to the non-western world. For example, he *discourages* cross-cultural workers to show the "Jesus Film" in parts of the world like Asia.[3] Despite the biblical and middle eastern setting of the film's content, it tends to view the gospel through a western lens and presents key elements of the gospel as viewed against a western backdrop. It does not take adequate account of the presuppositions and concerns of people who live in Asian cultures. Another example of a western approach to evangelism would be the use of the "Four Spiritual Laws," which was developed in North America and has been widely adopted in personal evangelism, particularly amongst students, in

---

[1] Michael Green, *Evangelism in the Early Church* (Rev. ed.) (Grand Rapids, MI: Eerdmans, 2003).
[2] Dean Flemming, *Contextualization in the New Testament: Patterns for Theology and Mission* (Downers Grove: InterVarsity Press, 2005), 315-318.
[3] Tom Steffen, "Don't Show the Jesus Film," *Evangelical Missions Quarterly* 29 (3) 1993:272-275.

the 1970s and 1980s. The "four spiritual laws" represent modern evangelicalism's response to people who hold to a modernist worldview. Can these approaches to evangelism be implemented in a completely different cultural and linguistic context with positive results? So much depends upon the context – in many Asian cultures, like Thailand, words like "God," "world," and "love," would all need careful explanation or possibly complete re-definition. Concepts like "sin" and "forgiveness" are also deeply embedded in the cultural setting. A critical assessment of all such approaches to evangelism is to be recommended and sometimes it is better to simply move to a completely new starting-point.

From the west to other parts of the world

Evangelists who use transplanted forms of evangelism are inadvertently assuming that the one gospel should be preached in the same way in every context in the world. The presentation of the gospel in this type of evangelism ends up being merely a translation of the content from one language to another with a total lack of contextualization of the meaning and significance of the message. The ease of global travel and the rise of short-term missions, has led to an increase in the number of Christians who cross cultural boundaries without understanding the significance of cultural difference. The north American scholar of missions, Ralph Winter has called the spread of this phenomenon the "re-amateurization" of missions.[4] Transplanted types of evangelism are also adopted by some Christians who live cross-culturally but are not prepared to learn local languages and do not take time to understand local customs and patterns of thought.

Evangelism across cultures

The problem of evangelistic approaches which are transplanted from foreign countries can be explained using a metaphor from gardening. Evangelistic approaches taken from the west to Asia, are like a potted plant which is transferred from a temperate culture to a tropical culture. The plant is expected to grow, mature and reproduce exactly as it did in the original culture, but the climate and environment have changed. It is better when doing contextualized evangelism to think of sharing the gospel in terms of planting "God's seed" in a new soil and allowing the seed to grow naturally, with time to adapt to its new setting and environment. In Christian terms, this means the gospel is given space to adapt to the

---

[4] Ralph Winter, "The Re-Amateurization of Missions," *Occasional Bulletin of the Evangelical Missiological Society* (Spring 1996), http://www.emsweb.org/ scholarship/23-occasional-bulletin-archives (accessed 22nd May 2012).

language, thought processes and rituals of the new culture without losing its kernel and core meanings.[5]

Problems occur when Thai Christians encounter a form of Christianity, from foreign Christians, that is not adequately contextualized. Although they have adopted Christianity at a formal, behavioural level, it will not have fully penetrated to the deeper level of their worldview.[6] By contrast, the most appropriate and relevant evangelism carefully considers the cultural contexts of the recipients of the Gospel. When the gospel is thoroughly contextualized, it engages people at the level of their deepest need. Evangelists who strive to find appropriate contextual forms of evangelism realize that both the presentation of the message and its form and structure must be adapted to the receptor culture. Although there is only *one* gospel, it can be perceived through different metaphors and different types of presentation.

Evangelism and the Context of the New Testament

When we look at the bible, we find that the noun "evangelism" does not occur in the Bible and the word "evangelist" is used only three times in the New Testament.[7] However, the concept of evangelism is strongly represented in the New Testament. The Greek word-groups that are used for evangelism are *euangelizo* (to share good news), *kerusso* (to preach), and *martureo* (to bear witness). The proclamation of Jesus' birth is one of the first examples of evangelism recorded in the New Testament as the angelic chorus bear witness to the good news: "Do not be afraid. I bring you good news that will cause great joy for all the people. Today in the town of David a Saviour has been born to you; he is the Messiah, the Lord." (Luke 2:10-11)

The New Testament itself offers an excellent example of contextualized evangelism in the character of the four gospels, which are in effect four contextualized versions of the one story:[8]

> Each of the four Gospels reflects the cultural orientation of its author and is clearly addressed to a particular audience. Matthew's Jewish orientation is reflected in his emphasis on messianic prophecy, kingship, the divine titles of

---

[5] Gailyn Van Rheenen, "Transplanted and Contextualized Churches," *Missology.org,* Monthly Missiological Reflection #17 (May 2001), http://www.missiology.org/MMR/mmr17.htm (accessed 22nd May 2012).

[6] Darrell Whiteman, "Contextualization: the Theory, the Gap and the Challenge," *International Bulletin of Missionary Research* 21(1) January 1997: 6.

[7] "Phillip is referred to as an evangelist (Acts 21:8), Timothy is exhorted to do the work of an evangelist (2 Tim 4:5), and we are told that some are called to be evangelists (Eph 4:11) (See Darius Salter, *American Evangelism* (Grand Rapids: Eerdmans, 1996), p.15.

[8] David Hesselgrave & Edward Rommen, *Contextualization: Meanings, Methods and Models* (Grand Rapids, MI: Baker, 1989), 8.

Jesus, and the Aramaisms which characterize his Jewish-Greek language. Luke, on the other hand, reflects a distinctly Hellenistic mind-set. ... The comprehensive range of Luke's gospel with its emphasis on the universal implications of the gospel gives it a unique appeal.

In the early church, evangelism was viewed in the "narrow sense of the verbal proclamation of the good news of salvation with a view of leading people to a right relationship with God through faith in Jesus Christ. But it touches on other aspects of "mission", which also includes the non-verbal aspects of Christian witness to non-Christians..."[9] Robert Coleman describes how Jesus viewed his role as evangelist: "Jesus interpreted his mission as fulfilment of this promise (Luke 4:18, 19). He saw himself as an evangelist, announcing the coming of the Kingdom of God. This message was to be proclaimed in the context of demonstrated compassion for the bruised and forgotten people of the world." As a result, Coleman cautions against truncated views of evangelism as either simply the verbal declaration of the gospel or simply caring for people and rectifying injustices in society. He prefers to see both activities as necessary elements of evangelism: "If Jesus had not borne the sorrows of people and performed deeds of mercy among them, we might question his concern. On the other hand, if he had not articulated the gospel, we would not have known why he came, nor how we could be saved."[10] The model of Jesus suggests that authentic evangelism that changes and transforms lives, requires more than talking about Four Spiritual Laws or just passing out gospel tracts. It is a message that needs to be fleshed out in word, deed and sign in ways that are relevant and meaningful for hearers in their own cultural context.

As the New Testament progresses from the Gospels to the book of Acts, we see that the task of evangelism passes on from the disciples, with their Jewish origins, to the wider church. The church is vividly portrayed as the missionary agent of God's redemptive plan of salvation. Jesus commanded the church to go into all the world and preach good news to all creation (Mark 16:15). The Holy Spirit came to empower the community of believers so that they can be powerful witnesses both locally and globally (Acts 1:8) which has implications for cross-cultural evangelism. In recent times, the Lausanne Covenant affirms the urgent need of evangelism through the church. In the church's mission of sacrificial service, evangelism is primary. World evangelization requires the whole church to take the whole gospel to the whole world. The church is at the very centre of God's cosmic purpose and is his appointed means of spreading the Gospel.[11] The purpose of the body of Christ is to present Jesus Christ in the

---

[9] Ralph Martin (ed.) *Dictionary of the Later New Testament and Its Developments* (Downers Grove, IL: Inter Varsity Press, 1997), 353.

[10] Robert Coleman, "Evangelism," in *Evangelical Dictionary of World Missions*, ed. Scott A. Moreau (Grand Rapids, MI: Baker Books, 2000), 343.

[11] John Stott (ed.), *Making Christ Known: Historic Mission Documents from the Lausanne Movement 1974-1989* (Cumbria: Paternoster Press, 1996).

world – tangible, real, visible and effective. For the church to do this in ways that are tangible and effective implies that in contexts like Asia, the church ought to proclaim a contextualized gospel.[12]

BOOK IDEA

> Flemming, Dean. *Contextualization in the New Testament: Patterns for Theology and Mission.* Downers Grove, IL: Inter Varsity Press, 2005.

This guide to contextualization looks carefully at the way in which the early church reaches out with the gospel to others. It starts with the cultures of the time, using the book of Acts as a backdrop; it considers the kind of sermons Paul preached; it looks at the kind of letters he wrote, all the time it asks questions about how the ideas and content connect to the intended audiences and how it reflects a process of shaping the gospel in context (83). The author draws on a high degree of biblical and theological understanding and is concerned to relate this to the practical realities of contextualization.

Contextualization and Evangelism – Practical Implications

In this section, we will look at a number of practical ways in which contextualization can be applied to evangelism. Enoch Wan has suggested how to reach out to contemporary Chinese people. He notes that Chinese cultural contexts put a stress on honour, harmony and relationships – precepts which are at the core of traditional Chinese cultural values.[13] Many countries like Thailand have significant Chinese populations and, even beyond such Chinese diaspora groups, these traditional cultural values are widely affirmed in societies across Asia. Harmonious relationships have more to do with people than ideas. To think of the gospel as a rational argument, presented in terms of linear logic, and proclamation, as in the traditional western approaches to evangelism, is to miss an important point when it comes to cultures in Asia. In cultures like Thailand, people put a stress on relationships and are concerned about the human messenger as well as the message.

The message of the gospel and the messenger

When it comes to evangelization amongst Thai people, the Christ-like character of the bearer of the Gospel (the messenger) and loving

---

[12] Charles Van Engen, *God's Missionary People: Rethinking the Purpose of the Local Church.* (Grand Rapid: Baker Books, 1991), 97.
[13] Enoch Wan, "Practical Contextualization: A Case Study of Evangelising Contemporary Chinese," *Global Missiology* October 2003, http://ojs. globalmissiology.org/index.php/english/issue/view/27 (accessed 4th June 2012).

relationships among believers, are as important as the life-changing reality of the gospel (the message), and are often a more powerful expression of Christianity. The common appeal of people in Thailand resonates with the statement, "Don't *tell* us the gospel but *show* us the gospel!" When the messenger is trustworthy and reliable, people are likely to listen to the message that the messenger is sharing. An authentic lifestyle (on the part of the messenger) when joined to a culturally appropriate method of proclaiming the gospel will definitely help to validate the content and power of the message.

Psychologists remind us that although every culture communicates through signal systems which include the verbal, written, and aural forms and so on, much of the information we receive and trust comes through seeing. The God of Israel frequently invited the Israelites to see God's goodness (Ps 34:8) and the works of God (Ps 66:5); Jesus also invited his disciples to "... come and you will see." (John 1:39). The best arena where those who are not members of the Christian community can see the authenticity of Christian life is in Christian homes, not in the church building on Sundays. One of the most important methods of spreading the gospel in antiquity was by the use of homes.[14] The *oikos* (home) in the New Testament and early church history is a place of mission where both Christians and non-Christians can experience genuine hospitality.[15] Throughout our church-planting experiences in Thailand, our home was a central place for all kinds of outreach and evangelism – we used it for events, for worship, for small groups, for media presentations, for sharing literature, and even for evangelism across the generations.[16]

During our focus on outreach, on Fridays, the house where each meeting was held would be full of joyful laughter: Thai people would be singing, praying, playing music and memorizing Bible verses. Our own home and our neighbours' homes have been a safe haven where people were able to talk freely, sharing their joys and sorrows, and where children could play without a care in front of their parents. Eating food together had a power to bring people close together regardless of religious belief. Once, we invited a typical elderly couple with their two daughters, who were initially quite suspicious of us due to our identity as Christians. Over a period of a few months, they observed us carefully; their concerns melted away and they were able to trust us. They cautiously opened their heart to what we shared. Finally, they accepted the message of the gospel through a "trustworthy messenger" and after eight months of baptismal classes, the whole family were baptized. The house church has been an effective strategy of

---

[14] Michael Green, *Evangelism in the Early Church* (Revised Edition) (Grand Rapids: Eerdmans, 2003).

[15] Roger Gehring, *House Church and Mission* (Grand Rapids: Eerdmans, 2004), 293.

[16] "Which Evangelism Approach should I use?" *Ministry Advantage* (Fuller Theological Seminary) 7 (3) Summer 1997: 6.

evangelism throughout church history and can be important for continuing generations who say that they like Jesus, but not the "church."

The message of the gospel and lifestyle

The messenger's lifestyle and its importance should also not be under-estimated. In recent years, Jim Chew has stressed the need for an appropriate lifestyle for cross-cultural workers that allows them to identify with local people.

The lifestyle of the messenger

Historically in Asia, there have been some notable examples of those who took contextualization seriously in terms of lifestyle. Robert de Nobili, an Italian Jesuit missionary to India, made it his objective to identify with those in the more elite "Brahmin" group. He built a hut in the Brahmin's quarter of the city, dressed like a Brahmin, declared himself to be a Roman rajah, and spread the Gospel to those of the Brahmin caste. In spite of some criticism, the Indian clergy recruited from Robert de Nobili proved to have high moral standards. Some became zealous and courageous missionaries.[17]

In China, in the 1860s, Hudson Taylor made similar efforts to identify with Chinese culture and adopted a contextualized lifestyle so that he could connect with Chinese people and help them realize that responding to the gospel and becoming a Christian did not mean abandoning Chinese culture.

Due to the increasing pace of globalization and urbanization, some facets of Asian life have been greatly transformed becoming more like the west. In urban settings, many Asians dress like westerners wearing a suit and tie rather than wearing more traditional clothes. Does this mean that Asians have been completely westernized? Not at all – like the proverbial iceberg, what lies beneath the surface of the outward appearance is a very Asian way of interacting with the world. Therefore, the need for a contextualized lifestyle for Asian Christian workers has not changed at all. In Thailand nowadays, cross-cultural workers in provincial towns like Chiang Mai need to be conscious of how a contextualized lifestyle translates into a lifestyle of service. The ultimate purpose of a contextualized lifestyle is to serve people effectively: it is not just about identifying with local people in cultural ways. In the same way that the incarnate Jesus identified with people – using the local dialect, local dress and local food to serve people effectively – the urgent call for missionaries working in Asia is to identify deeply with the people of their target culture. The first step in building deep relationships with local people is to learn to speak their language really well; identifying with them in daily matters

---

[17] Kenneth Latourette, *History of Christianity.* (Vol. 2) (N.Y.: Harper & Row, 1953), 931-932.

helps to build trust, and this allows for relationships to be formed and gives opportunities for the gospel to be heard in Asian contexts.

The message of the gospel and the hearer – scriptures and concepts

The Christians scriptures translated into a local language, the heart language of the hearers, is an essential starting-point for effective evangelism. A clear presentation of the gospel goes beyond simply translating the words of the Scriptures into a local language. The use of Christian ideas and concepts which we are familiar with may need to be adjusted for our hearers to understand what we are saying. The early Church Fathers were skilful at presenting the Gospel to the Greco-Roman people of their day. Justin Martyr tried to establish a contact point using the terms and concepts that already existed in Greco-Roman culture to explain theological ideas. He chose "logos," a platonic term for word, truth, and wisdom connected to what was "good" to explain about Jesus.[18] In pagan contexts, Justin explored the relationship between Stoic love and Christian love believing that cultural values can be perfected in Christ. He borrowed from platonic philosophy to contextualize the gospel in order to convey truth to pagan Greco-Roman citizens. In Jewish contexts, Justin used the fulfilment of prophecy to describe Jesus. Justin started with where the audiences were by identifying the common ground or experiences. He quoted the Scriptures extensively, but their message was woven into conversation that was easy to follow and fitted the interests and thought patterns of his hearers.

In Asian contexts, one crucial element, usually omitted in sharing the Gospel, is the presence of spirits and the spirit world: many Asians relate to spirits in their daily life and are fearful of spirits – which are termed "evil spirits" in some Asian languages. Effective proclamation of the gospel to Asian peoples has to deal with this issue. Asians want to know how the gospel of Jesus helps them deal with spirits. A Thai woman of high education performed many religious activities to appease spirits through amulets, charms, spirit houses, and so on. After building a close relationship with her and her young daughter, we thought that she had clearly understood the gospel and was ready to accept it, but we discovered that this was not the case: the gospel that we had presented to her did not adequately deal with her fear of spirits. Eventually, after many months of drawing on the living word of the Bible, and following prayers to cast out spirits, she was ready to accept Christ. Even after her acceptance of the gospel, it took several months before she experienced freedom in Christ, having turned from the power of spirits. Asians generally want to know

---

[18] Thomas Falls (ed.), *Saint Justin Martyr* (New York: Christian Heritage, 1949), 38.

what Christianity has to say about spirits and the power of darkness, this forms an important part of a contextualized gospel.

Suggested Reading on Cross-Cultural Evangelism

Chew, J. *When You Cross Cultures*. (Rev. ed.) Singapore: Navigators, 2009.
Dowsett, R. (ed.) *Global Mission: Reflections and Case Studies*. Pasadena, CA: William Carey, 2010.
Hollinghurst, S. *Mission Shaped Evangelism: The Gospel in Contemporary Culture*. Norwich: Canterbury Press, 2010.

Meekness – an approach to lifestyle in Thailand

Nanthachai Mejudhon,[19] a Thai missiologist, has been advocating "meekness" as an effective contextualized approach to reach out to Thai Buddhists. Sharing the gospel with Thai people through the use of meekness is an approach to evangelism that is opposed to the more direct, pushy, even aggressive approaches that characterize some western styles. For effective evangelism amongst Thai people, Christians have to develop long-term, genuine, sincere relationships with Buddhists with "no strings attached," and have a humble attitude towards Buddhism and Thai culture. In the Thai context, the message of the Scriptures needs to connect with the distinctive thought patterns and perspectives of the Thai people.

The message of the gospel and the hearer – preaching

The apostle Paul, with his passionate preaching, paved the way for the gospel to spread in the major cities of the Eastern Roman Empire. Proclamation of God's word was a key factor when there were mass conversions of people. "… faith comes from hearing the message…" (Rom 10:17). Due to a lack of background knowledge of the Bible, many Asians, like earlier citizens of the Roman empire, have to hear the message over and over again before they can clearly comprehend the message of the gospel. The development of the "3/300 Mission" of the Kachin Baptist Convention in Myanmar in the late 1970s is a good example of the power of preaching. This special event was organized by Kachin Baptists to mobilize three hundred young evangelists between 1979 and 1981. The evangelists entered towns and villages and their ministry resulted in over 7600 baptisms.[20] Their main method of evangelism was open-air preaching

---

[19] Nanthachai Mejudhon. *Meekness: A New Approach to Christian Witness to the Thai People* Unpublished Doctor of Missiology Thesis, Asbury Theological Seminary, Wilmore, Kentucky, U.S.A., 1997.
[20] Sau Hkaw, "3/300 Mission of Kachin Baptist Convention." Unpublished Master's Thesis, Burma Institute of Theology, Yangon, Myanmar, 1990, 114.

both in urban and in rural areas; in addition to preaching, healing ministry was carried out at prisons, hospitals and homes.

This raises the question of whether preaching alone can bring people to Christ. One may proclaim the gospel earnestly but do so in such a way that the hearers do not really understand the message and as a result this may not produce genuine fruit in people's lives. I have seen eager short-term visitors present the gospel on many occasions without considering the context or its cultural characteristics. Sometimes the gospel is preached without an adequate knowledge of the Thai language and the disposition of the hearers: such evangelism can actually hinder further opportunities to share the gospel in a more meaningful way. A few weeks of friendly behaviour do not guarantee the trust of local people. Premature or inadvertently coerced commitments to Christ can often turn a person away rather than help them make a genuine commitment.

Some evangelicals from both America and Asia have tended to reduce the meaning of Christian faith to a narrow understanding of conversion and have often shared the gospel in ways that are perceived as "aggressive" by Asian people. We have frequently witnessed short-term mission teams and evangelistic programmes portraying a form of Christianity that is little more than a call to conversion. For Asians, repeating a prayer to accept the gospel after raising their hands does not usually have any significant implications. Simply out of cultural courtesy to foreigners, many of them tend to raise their hands at such evangelistic meetings. A mission team from Korea once enthusiastically preached the gospel at a local university in Chiang Mai and team members were so excited when some Thai students prayed a short prayer to receive Christ. Later, when other Christians who were based locally, followed-up on what had happened, they found that the students had no idea of what accepting the gospel really meant.

Contextualization and Evangelism – Wider Issues

Surprisingly, very few books on evangelism promote the concept of models of *evangelism* that can be reproduced. However, such models are an important aspect of forms of evangelism that can be contextualized in cultures like Thailand. A revival that lasts only one generation will not have a lasting impact. In the west, significant churches of the past collect dust or are converted into buildings that have a different secular focus. Movements that start from grass-root Christians and local communities can last longer and make a greater impact on the world.

The parable of the kernel of wheat (John 12:24) that Jesus shared, not only teaches us about the need for sacrifice in order to bear fruit, but also the urgency of the cycle of regeneration. A living tree will bear its fruit and in turn will need to be buried in the ground and produce another generation of fruits. Michael Wilkins points out that becoming a disciple of Jesus

Christ is based around a three-fold process: through regeneration a person becomes a new creation in God; this new identity is granted to the person who accepts Christ in his life; regeneration takes place at the time of conversion and is worked out in the activities of life. The first process has to do with abiding in the Word of God; the second has to do with loving others by belonging in the community of Christ; and the third has to do with bearing fruits by sharing the Gospel.[21]

The need for models of evangelism which can be reproduced by local communities

In order to develop a model of evangelism and discipleship that can be reproduced, it is important to start with the local Christian community. This local community plays a vital role in modelling Christian life. It is the local Christian community that will attract those who do not believe to Christ. The community of believers needs to be accountable to each other for spiritual growth – only living organisms can reproduce themselves. As the maturity of the community of believers develops, the local community becomes a sending body from its very own neighbourhood right to the ends of the earth. Representatives of the community take with them the message of the Good News that has been nurtured and developed in the community's own life. The living body of Christ will be manifested in the unity of the Christian community. Ajith Fernando[22] addresses the importance of unity in the Christian community as follows: "We can affirm that in Christ we are one, and through the church we can present a model of integration and harmony. This becomes a point of hope in a gloomy situation of mistrust and strife." Rather than focusing on models or methods of evangelism that can be reproduced, we ought to focus on creating a community of genuine believers which can demonstrate living discipleship and so reproduce effective evangelism amongst other communities.

God's sovereignty and the place of prayer in relation to evangelism

We have looked at ways in which evangelism can be shaped by human reflection on culture and the gospel in the context of a country like Thailand. In a similar way, we can take more proactive steps to discern the trends and social dynamics of the world we live in. In our era of accessible information and information technology, we can study world trends and learn about places where God is at work, and what we learn from this can

---

[21] Michael Wilkins, *Following the Master* (Grand Rapids, MI: Zondervan, 1992), 238.

[22] Ajith Fernando, "The Church: the Mirror of the Trinity," in *Global Missiology for the 21st Century*, ed.William Taylor (Grand Rapids, MI: World Evangelical Fellowship, 2000), 255.

help us share the gospel in an effective way in cultures where the church is still in a minority. We should remember, however, that the sudden responsiveness of people to the gospel (as in the rise of Christian people movements) cannot simply be explained in human terms. It is part of the divine mystery of the gospel and its administration as to how a sudden breakthrough can happen in an environment that seemed to be disinterested or even resistant to the Gospel. God's sovereignty alone sets the stage for the work of mission.

We can reflect on what this means for church leaders and mission partners. In part, it means that we should certainly intercede on behalf of people groups and nations for God's divine intervention. The first church in Jerusalem started its outreach and mission to the surrounding areas and later to the world, by praying for the empowerment of the Holy Spirit after the one hundred and twenty followers of Jesus joined together as a group (Acts 1:12-14). Prayer is one of the most important elements in evangelism. In response to prayer from believers, God removes barriers that hinder people from hearing and seeing the good news of the gospel. Dr. Hardie, a Canadian medical missionary, had laboured for a decade on the Korean peninsula without seeing much in the way of visible results. In this context of frustration, he joined with seven other missionaries in 1903 and they gathered for prayer, confessed their short-comings before Korean congregations and continued fervently in prayer. After a few months, Korean Christians caught the same passion for prayer, confessed their sins and joined the foreign Christians in prayer. This was the background to the Pyong Yang Revival in 1907 that led to thousands of new converts and a hundred years of active church life in Korea.[23] Corporate prayer can create a great wave of passion which pushes the church to reach out to those who do not know or believe the gospel. Paul reminds Christians, "And pray in the Spirit on all occasions with all kinds of prayers and requests. With this in mind, be alert and always keep on praying for all the Lord's people." (Eph 6:18) Christians should spend time in praying for others, prayer ought to be set free from church building and the church ought to take its prayer to homes, streets, markets, towns and cities. Every believer's home should be transformed to become a house of prayer.

Finally, we should remember that another aspect of the divine mystery of the administration of the gospel, is the fact that some Christians will toil diligently, like many of those who have worked in Thailand (as in an earlier generation in Korea), who never saw the time of blessing but who gave their life to the work of evangelism in another culture, in the hope of a day when multitudes of people from the culture where they served will come to know Christ.

---

[23] Elmer Towns and Douglas Porter, *The Ten Greatest Revivals Ever* (Ann Arbor, MI: Servant Publications, 2000), 44.

Conclusion

In our modern generation, people are moving in increasing numbers from rural to urban areas: more than 45% of the world's population lives in urban areas; by 2025, it may increase to be 60% of the population. The next frontier for evangelism does not lie in the remote jungles or small villages but in the mega-cities where people from all walks of life are congregating. In Asia, with some two billion people and around a third of the world's population, the number of large urban cities continues to rise and, in countries like Thailand, this presents us with increasing challenges of learning how to contextualize the gospel in urban centres. Urban evangelism is one of the greatest tasks that the church of Christ will encounter in the 21st century.

The principles which have been outlined in this chapter will help to give a foundation to those who seek to work in a country like Thailand as they recognize the importance of taking account of culture and as they engage in the task of evangelism. We can be encouraged in our efforts by the writings of the American historian, Philip Jenkins[24] (and others) who have described how the church in the majority world, contrary to the expectation of many in the west, is growing and emerging in the most unlikely of places. The new growth of Christianity that is taking place in the countries of the majority world is producing a church which is dynamic and which holds to the orthodox theological and ethical traditions of the church universal. If we adopt principles of contextualization in our work of evangelism in other cultures, then we can share in this process of making the gospel known in ways that are effective and that usher in the growth of new and living communities of disciples who will in their turn model a vibrant and vital expression of Christian faith.

Questions For Reflection/Discussion

1. Why might evangelists *avoid* "the Jesus Film" and "the four spiritual laws" in a country like Thailand? What does the author see as a *better* model for evangelism?
2. What are some of the ways in which the *lifestyle* of the messenger is important (and can be considered as *part* of the message)?
3. What can we learn from Justin Martyr's method of finding a "contact point"? What modern Thai example does the author suggest illustrates such an approach? Why does he see it as significant?

---

[24] Philip Jenkins, *The Next Christendom* (New York: Oxford University Press, 2002), 93.

CONTEXTUALIZATION AND DISCIPLESHIP

Minho Song

Minho Song shows that the connection between culture and discipleship is a neglected area in studies of contextual theology. He reckons that many people who cross cultures to engage in ministry often fail to give enough attention to the character of discipleship training and the content of the materials which they use. Song suggests a deeper engagement with local culture and worldview, outlining elements that need to be enhanced or altered in any cultural engagement with the gospel. He develops a practical approach in four steps: 1) take account of biblical emphases relevant to all cultures; 2) recognize the specific character of each cultural context; 3) be prepared to create relevant materials and, finally, 4) give due consideration to the settings in which teaching takes place and its ethos in any given culture.

Contextual theology has gained significant momentum in recent theological studies. Historically, theological reflection centred around two sources, scripture and tradition, but now it is virtually impossible to engage in a meaningful theological discussion without taking seriously the third source: context. Stephen Bevans argues that "doing theology contextually is not an option... [but] is a theological imperative."[1] Understanding the context of a particular people means to appreciate their culture and history as well as the issues currently impacting their lives.

As a Korean Canadian who has also lived and worked in the Philippines, my experiences in ministry with Asian peoples like Koreans (with their very distinctive cultural identity), and with other cultural groups in the Philippines has shown me that it is critical to take account of context as we engage in mission and as we seek to help people become disciples in Asian contexts. We need to build on the historical and theoretical work which has gone before to develop a more effective way of making disciples in Asia.

Towards the end of the 19th century, many mission agencies accepted Rufus Anderson and Henry Venn's "three-self" model as a guideline for their church planting projects. In order to promote the rapid growth of autonomous churches, missionaries encouraged the emerging churches to be self-supporting, self-propagating and self-governing. Nowadays, however, such a model is considered inadequate because of its lack of emphasis on the receptor's context. It is argued that even the theology of the emerging church must be self-generated, hence the term "fourth self" of

---

[1] Stephen Bevans, *Models of Contextual Theology* (Rev. and exp. ed.) (Maryknoll, NY: Orbis, 2002), 3.

self-theologizing became important.[2] If context is ignored, the church runs the risk of being seen as a foreign enterprise with a foreign message.[3] Dean Gilliland defines contextualized theology as:

> ... the dynamic reflection carried out by the particular church upon its own life in light of the Word of God and historic Christian truth. Guided by the Holy Spirit, the church continually challenges, incorporates, and transforms elements of the cultural milieu, bringing these under the lordship of Christ. As members of the body of Christ interpret the Word, using their own thoughts and employing their own cultural gifts, they are better able to understand the gospel as incarnation.[4]

We must consider at least two important points raised by Gilliland in this definition. Firstly, he emphasizes the importance of the church's self-theologizing, "upon its *own* life... using *own* thoughts and employing their (the church members') *own* cultural gifts..." (emphasis mine). The task of communicating the gospel message in a culturally meaningful and relevant way ultimately belongs to the national church, to its national leadership and to all the members of the church. Even though this task begins in the hands of missionaries, missionaries must look ahead and empower the national leaders so that eventually they will do their own theologizing.[5] Secondly, Gilliland speaks of bringing "elements of the cultural milieu under the lordship of Christ." It is the church that must "challenge, incorporate and transform" the elements of culture so as to bring these under the lordship of Christ. Contextualization must be understood in a comprehensive manner, covering not only the areas of Bible translation, the expressions of worship, leadership structure, and so on, but also the very fabric of believers' commitment to and involvement in society as *disciples* of Jesus Christ. In that regard, contextualization and discipleship are two concepts that cannot be separated.

---

[2] Paul Hiebert, *Anthropological Insights for Missionaries* (Grand Rapids, MI: Baker, 1985), 195-196.

[3] Douglas Howard, "Measuring Contexualization in Church and Missions," *International Journal of Frontier Missions*, 12(3) 1995: 135.

[4] Dean Gilliland, "Contextual Theology as Incarnation Mission" in *The Word Among Us: Contextualizing Theology for Mission Today,* ed. Dean Gilliland (Waco: Word, 1989), 12-13. For a brief historical survey on the term "contextualization," see Bruce Nicholls, *Contextualization: a Theology of Gospel and Culture* (Downers Grove, IL: Inter Varsity Press, 1979), 20-36. For an Asian evangelical response to the concerns raised in the contextualization debate, see Bong Rin Ro, "Contextualization: Asian Theology" in *Biblical Theology in Asia,* ed. Ken Gnanakan (Bangalore: Theological Book Trust, 1995), 3-17.

[5] This is particularly the case in countries like Cambodia, which was ravaged by the civil war and the genocide of Khmer Rouge (1975-79) during which most church leaders lost their lives. More concerted efforts are needed on the part of the missionaries working in Cambodia to raise up future theologians and writers who can reflect their own situation and give direction for the Cambodian church.

Discipleship and Contextualization

Discipleship is often overlooked in the discussion of contextualization. Generally speaking, missiologists and missionaries pay attention to the initial communication of the gospel and try to ensure that their message is receptor-centred. When it comes to follow-up and discipling new believers, however, the approaches taken are not as systematic or well-thought through. How does one disciple a Muslim background believer? How does one disciple a Buddhist background believer? What about people coming from the urban slums of Manila or from a Communist regime? If we are careful about how we present the Gospel message for the first time hearers, then we should also be careful about how we present the follow-up and discipleship materials for those who desire to grow closer to Jesus Christ. The next two examples illustrate the problem, raised in this chapter, that discipleship is often overlooked in the discussion of contextualization.

When I was at a discipleship seminar at a church in Korea several years ago, I met a Christian worker who was evangelizing and discipling people from North Korea who had escaped to China from North Korea. When asked how he designed his discipleship program, he simply replied that he uses the materials developed by some churches in Seoul. In his mind, the choice of such a material posed no problem since "the language is the same for North and South Koreans." I had a similar conversation with a missionary from another country working in the Philippines. He was excited to share that he had just secured the copyright of the discipleship lessons used by a mega-church in Southern California. He planned to translate these lessons into *Tagalog* (the main language of the Philippines) and offer them at an affordable price to churches in the Philippines. I responded courteously, but I was concerned that this was not really appropriate. These two examples illustrate a lack of care on our part in not taking seriously the role of context in cross-cultural discipleship. Even though most missionaries are aware of the term "contextualization," in reality there exists a big gap between theory and practice.

Discipleship in context is an application of contextual theology in following up and discipling new believers in a cross-cultural setting. It takes the receptor's context seriously. It acknowledges, first of all, the simple and obvious fact that no one comes to Jesus Christ in a spiritual vacuum. It rejects the assumption that the mind of the receptor is a *tabula rasa*, (an empty slate), ready to receive everything the missionary has to teach about spirituality without their being any clash with, or accommodation to, the existing set of beliefs. Discipleship in context is based on the recognition that everyone has been captive to their own spiritual or religious orientation before coming to know Christ (see Eph 2:1-3 and Mark 8:20-23). The receptor's mind is far from empty or free. Rather, the mind must go through a fierce battle for biblical truths to be written on it.

Going back to the example cited earlier, we can see how the discipleship lessons developed by a church in Southern California are not suitable in a Filipino context. In the Philippines, evangelical churches are quick to adopt a discipleship program or a Bible study series popularized in the West. However, because the material was not written with the Filipino audience in mind, it does not take into account the spiritual and social dimensions of the Filipino mind. The material does not touch the deeper structures of the Filipino worldview and psyche. Discipling a new believer, who comes from a nominal Catholic background, requires a concerted effort to speak to the Filipino mind and heart.

Discipleship and the Filipino Mindset

Top Level	Evangelical teaching on discipleship
Middle Level	Catholic tradition and practices (nominal)
Bottom Level	Animistic beliefs and assumptions

The task of discipling Filipinos in their context requires us to examine the values and assumptions that the new believers bring with them. Lessons on discipleship must penetrate the bottom level where people's animistic beliefs and assumptions can be challenged and transformed in obedience to scripture. Such an effort minimizes syncretism and encourages faithfulness to biblical truth.[6] Ultimately, a call to discipleship is a call to adopt a biblical worldview. Our task of discipling is to call people to the biblical worldview of truth. For this to happen, there must be a violent clash of two worldviews, the receptor's and that of the Bible. Sometimes, the task is compounded by the presence of another worldview brought in by the missionary. Melba Maggay[7] writes:

> Christianity in the Philippines is a "sandwich religion," a layer of Christian beliefs piled on top of a largely pagan slice of bread. We have yet to communicate in a way that truly wrestles with the people's worldview. We need to locate the Gospel at those precise points where Filipino mythology and worldview differ from those of the West.

Discipleship in context rises out of a dynamic interplay between text (passed down by tradition) and context. By paying attention to both the Bible and the context in which people live, we are then able to bring the

---

[6] In the same way, discipling North Korean believers requires a deep level understanding of their life under communism. For more than half a century, they have been indoctrinated with atheism. One wonders just how meaningful the statement "God loves you" is to a North Korean refugee hearing for the first time about a supreme being who is loving and personal.

[7] Melba Maggay, *The Gospel in Filipino Context* (Manila: OMF Literature, 1987), 4.

task of disciple-making in a *culturally relevant* and *biblically faithful* manner. For disciple-making to be effective, it must be grounded in the appropriate context in which people live. It is the context that allows us to understand the needs and issues of the new believers. Only after these needs and issues are properly identified and understood, can we then begin to design a curriculum that will help people to follow Jesus faithfully in their context. In short, borrowing discipleship materials or approaches used in another context ought to be resisted. Instead, national leadership must be encouraged and empowered to design their own curricula and approaches to disciple the new believers.

BOOK IDEA

> Acoba, E. (et al). *Doing Theology in the Philippines.* Manila: OMF Literature, 2005.

The authors in this book interact with two sets of themes. Firstly, they reflect about "contextualization" itself – they show the role of the bible in shaping contextual theology; they show how contexts shape our understanding of ministry; they engage in a quest to do contextualization "from within." Secondly, they relate contextual theology to several aspects of the life of discipleship – the spirit-world, the problem of evil, political involvement, spirituality, worship and the catechism. This material would be relevant for audiences in South East Asia and beyond.

Discipleship Without Context

Each context presents a different set of challenges for followers of Jesus Christ. We can see this difference by comparing the context of the book of Revelation with the context of the book of Matthew. In the book of Revelation, John defines "disciples" as those who "*follow* the Lamb wherever he goes" (Rev 14:4). They are the ones who persevere right to the end and come to the wedding supper of the Lamb by overcoming the world.[8] To come out as victor, the followers of the Lamb must face the following two challenges:

---

[8] If we take the late dating of Revelation, the book of Revelation was written to the seven churches faced with the emperor cult (the worship of the emperor). These churches in Asia Minor adopted the emperor cult enthusiastically, '… possibly more than elsewhere in the Roman Empire' (I. Beasley-Murray, "Revelation, Book of," in *Dictionary of the Later New Testament and Its Developments,* ed. Ralph Martin, and Peter H. Davids (Downers Grove, IL: Inter Varsity Press, 1997), 1028. Domitian was perhaps the worst of all emperors as he demanded that people address him as *dominus et deus* (Lord and God). As for the Christians, the pressure to avoid the emperor cult was compounded by the pressure coming from traditional religious cults. Together, they asked for a concrete response from the believers.

1. the relentless force of seduction by "Babylon" with all its glamour and charm, which is nothing but deception and destruction – the churches at Ephesus, Pergamum, Sardis, Thyatira and Laodicea were warned against this;
2. the fierce persecution by the Beast which, in no ambiguous terms, demands worship from people – the churches at Smyrna and Philadelphia did not to fall prey to this force and were commended by Jesus in turn.

John writes that seduction and persecution, the twin evils designed to elicit apostasy from the believers, will climax at the end. He urges the believers to live godly and faithful lives right to the end and arrive safely at the wedding supper of the Lamb. In John's context, to follow Jesus means to overcome the world at all personal cost:

> Yet you have a few people in Sardis who have not soiled their clothes. They will walk with me, dressed in white, for they are worthy. 5 The one who is victorious will, like them, be dressed in white. I will never blot out the name of that person from the book of life, but will acknowledge that name before my Father and his angels. (Rev 3:4-5)

Discipleship in John's context is different from discipleship in the context of Matthew's community. The main problem with the Matthean community was their group identity as God's people. Mostly composed of Jewish stock, the Matthean community stood at a crossroads faced with the choice of insisting on Jewish identity and facing extinction or enlarging their tent by reaching out to the Gentiles. Mission to the Gentiles was Matthew's answer to this community in crisis. Mission was used as a form of discipleship. The gospel of Matthew was written "… not to compose a life of Jesus but to provide guidance to a community in crisis."[9] Discipleship in John's context meant resisting seduction and enduring persecution: discipleship in Matthew's context meant letting go of one's identity and accepting God's plan for a new identity. We can see from these biblical examples that it is the context that determines the issues of discipleship. The text (the Bible) teaches us *whom* to follow while the context teaches us *how* to follow Jesus. Needless to say, when we use transferable or generic discipleship material, we miss out the important issues of a particular context that stand in the way of discipleship.

In the Philippines context, it is easy to identify corruption as one of the critical issues facing discipleship. Corruption is a way of life, rampant in every sector of the Filipino society.[10] It stands in the way of the believer's

---

[9] David Bosch, *Transforming Mission* (Maryknoll: Orbis, 1991), 57.

[10] The Philippines ranks 4th from the worst, in Asia, out of 15 Asian countries rated and 92nd in the world in the Corruption Perception Index 2002 according to Transparency International. The country has the dubious distinction of having two of the top ten corrupt heads of the government in the world, those of Ferdinand Marcos (1972-86) and Joseph Estrada (1998-2001). See Transparency International.

spiritual maturity. Evelyn Miranda-Feliciano draws attention to "a trilogy of manoeuvres" deeply ingrained in the Filipino psyche, *lusot, lakad* and *lagay*. She defines them as follows:

1. *lusot* means to escape from something by wriggling into a hole or through a slit;
2. *lakad* literally means "walk"; a euphemism for making an attempt to smooth out difficulties by using a network of "connections";
3. *lagay* means money to smooth over a situation, money set aside for illegal gambling or a bribe, plain and simple.[11]

For those who seriously desire to follow Jesus Christ in the Philippines, they must deal with the problem of corruption. There are two important questions: 1) how do I stay pure from corruption? and 2) how do I help transform this society from corruption? To quote Miranda-Feliciano, "How truly honest can a Christian be in a culture that has accepted *lusot, lakad* and *lagay* as a system operating outside legal and official policies?"[12] A discipleship material designed for a Southern California middle class church does not cover corruption since it is not a pressing issue for the believers there. Hence, by adopting a material intended for Southern California, the discipler conveniently overlooks the critical issues of discipleship in the Philippines altogether.[13]

We can also talk about other critical issues in discipleship such as the residue of folk Catholic beliefs. They need to be brought out into the open and evaluated as the new believer makes a fresh start in following Jesus wholeheartedly. There are also social values like *pakikisama* and *utang na loob* which are not bad in and of themselves, but which can be used to hamper Christian growth in the Philippines context.[14] These values need to be discussed and transformed in service of the Kingdom of God. If they are not discussed, disciple-making will remain superficial and people's deep-level assumptions and beliefs will go unchallenged.

Global Corruption Report 2004: Special Focus: Political Corruption. London: Pluto Press, 2004.

[11] Evelyn Miranda-Feliciano, *Filipino Values and Our Christian Faith* (Manila: OMF Literature, 1990), 2-5.

[12] Miranda-Feliciano, *Filipino Values*, 6.

[13] For recent theological critique of this issue in South-East Asia, see also Hwa Yung. *Bribery and Corruption: Biblical Reflections and Case Studies for the Marketplace in Asia* (Singapore: Graceworks, 2010).

[14] These words refer to Filipino social values connected to "obligation": *pakikisama* – a strong sense of obligation from relational ties (like those of family); *utang na loob* – the sense of obligation that comes from having received favours from others.

Further Reading on Contextualization in the Philippines

de Mesa, J. "Doing Theology as Inculturation in the Asian Context." In *New Directions in Mission and Evangelisation. (Vol 3.) Faith and Culture* edited by J.A. Scherer, and S. B. Bevans, 117-133. Maryknoll, NY: Orbis, 1999.

Hwa Yung. *Bribery and Corruption: Biblical Reflections and Case Studies for the Marketplace in Asia.* Singapore: Graceworks, 2010.

Maggay, M. *A Clash of Culture: Early American Protestant Missions and Filipino Religious Consciousness.* Manila: Anvil, 2011.

Maggay, M. *Jew to the Jew and Greek to the Greek: Reflections on Culture and Globalization.* Manila: ISACC, 2001.

Maggay, M. *The Gospel in Culture: Contextualization Issues through Asian Eyes.* Manila: ISACC and OMF Literature, 2013.

Steps in Contextual Discipleship

How then does one enter into another's culture and engage in a cross-cultural discipleship process? I will now propose several steps involved in contextual discipleship. Before we take the first step, we must first identify our own theological convictions about contextualization. Stephen Bevans[15] discusses six models of contextual theology in his book *Models of Contextual Theology*: the Translation model, the Anthropological model, the Praxis model, the Synthetic model, the Transcendental model and the Countercultural model. Of the six, three are of particular importance to us:

> 1) *the translation model* starts with the text – it assumes that there is essential doctrine that transcends culture and transcends context; this essential doctrine is put into other terms in a way that the receptor can understand (also referred to as accommodation);

> 2) *the anthropological model* starts with the context – the present human situation is the focus of divine revelation as much as scripture and tradition have been the foci of divine revelation in the past; thus one needs to attend and listen to God's presence in the present context (also known as indigenization).

> 3) *the synthetic model* believes in the universality of Christian faith – however, it does not define the constant in Christian identity narrowly in a set of propositions; each context has its own distinctiveness to work out the universality of Christian faith; thus, theology is a reflection of the context in the light of the text (alternatively called the dialogical model).

In advocating discipleship in context, I propose that we choose a model of contextual theology that pays due attention to both text and context. Of course, we must begin with text, the revealed Word of God. The core message has to do with the redemptive work of God in Christ. One thing we must keep in mind is that the existing category of Christian theology (the typical order of western systematic theology) is not necessarily the best arrangement for people in other contexts. Thinking so is tantamount to

---

[15] Bevans, *Models of Contextual Theology.*

ignoring the context. The following approach to contextual discipleship utilizes the strength of the translation model and the synthetic model. In coming up with a contextualized discipleship material in a particular context, one must take the following steps:

1. state the message of the Bible that transcends culture
2. identify the needs and issues of the context
3. create one's own discipleship material
4. determine the best pedagogical approach to the context

1) state the contextual message of the Bible that transcends cultures

We do not need to start everything from scratch; that would be not only a waste of time but also a show of arrogance that God could not teach us through the findings of others. There are biblical truths or themes that transcend all cultures and contexts. These have been already identified, deposited and passed down through two thousand years of church history (tradition) although we may disagree on how they are arranged. Nonetheless, the essential, message of the Bible that transcends cultures can be agreed upon, as reflected, for instance, in the Lausanne Covenant.[16]

While I consider the interaction of text and context essential, I am not assuming that both text and context are culturally conditioned and relative to each other.[17] I believe that there is a message in the Bible, that transcends cultures and contexts which has to do with the redemptive work of the triune God. This work is carried out in the world through the obedience of God's people (church). The following are the six essential biblical themes that I have identified: they make up the message of the Bible that transcends contexts.[18] These themes in turn interact with the issues raised in a particular context. Naturally, people in one context understand each Bible theme differently from those in another context.

Step two: 2) identify the needs and issues of the context

The needs and issues of a particular context must be identified in so far as they have a bearing on the task of discipling new believers. In other words, we need to ask, "What are the issues that stand in the way of the new believers from becoming mature disciples of Jesus Christ?" We can start with more obvious issues and move down to subtle ones. For example, one of the obvious challenges facing churches in Burma-Myanmar is folk

---

[16] Lausanne Committee on World Evangelization. "The Lausanne Covenant." www.lausanne.org/en/documents/lausanne-covenant.html (accessed 22nd May 2012).

[17] Bruce Nicholls, *Contextualization*, 24-25.

[18] The number of the themes can vary, depending on how one regroups them.

Buddhism. It is so prevalent in Burmese culture that a new believer in Christ must make a clean break from his past if he is going to mature in Christ. In my visit to the homes of Burman people in Yangon City, I have consistently seen two altars in their living room, a spirit house for Buddha and *payasin* (a spirit house) for *nagana* (the local spirit or *nat*). While Buddha takes care of them after life, *nagana* guides and protects them in this life.[19] Their religion (folk Buddhism) is a harmonious response to these two sources of protection.

Six Biblical Themes that Transcend Cultures

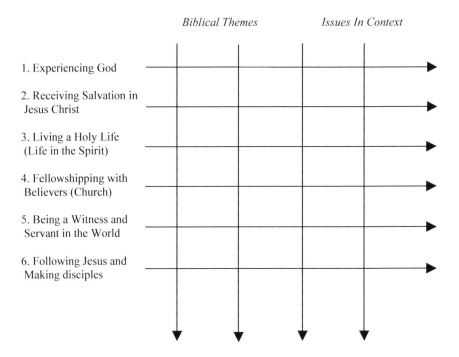

Biblical Themes   *Issues In Context*

1. Experiencing God

2. Receiving Salvation in Jesus Christ

3. Living a Holy Life (Life in the Spirit)

4. Fellowshipping with Believers (Church)

5. Being a Witness and Servant in the World

6. Following Jesus and Making disciples

A Burmese pastor told me that most new believers are still afraid of throwing out the altars when they become Christians due not only to a fear of the spirits but also the fear of rejection by family and neighbours. When I visited a local Christian bookstore in Yangon in order to look for

---

[19] His name is *Maung Tin Tae* and is known as 'the Lord of the Great Mountain.' According to the legend, the king, afraid of the power of *Maugn Tin Tae*, a strong blacksmith, burned him to death. So people today offer coconut and red cloth to him regularly. See D. Senapatiratne, S. Allen and R. Bowers, *Folk Buddhism in Southeast Asia* (Pnomh Phen: Training of Timothys, 2003), 22-23.

discipleship materials, I was not able to find a single book that addressed the topic of folk Buddhism. Instead, what I found was straight-forward translations of discipleship materials by western groups like the Navigators and other para-church groups. Needless to say, in the Burmese context, part of discipling new believers includes giving instructions on how to make a break with the idols, both physically and spiritually – that is why identifying the needs and issues of the Burmese context is the first step in helping believers become serious followers of Jesus Christ.

Issues and Needs in the Filipino Context

If one were to examine the Filipino context, the following issues and needs would be part of the list:

- debilitating fear of spirits[20]
- notions about God, Church, the Gospel, the Bible, prayer and so on that need to be brought into line with biblical teaching (influenced by nominal beliefs in folk Catholicism)
- extreme family obligations and other excessive demands on relationships (pakikisama wrongly applied)
- immoral living, drinking, gambling and other social ills
- corruption (pandaraya) at all levels of society and other societal and environmental problems
- lack of material resources (dire poverty)
- an increasing gap between the rich and the poor

Issues such as those above need to be identified and studied. Ultimately, we need to understand these issues from the perspective of the Filipino worldview. While we ought to pay attention to the critical issues present in a particular context, we must also identify the *positive* aspects of context that make the task of discipleship easier. For example, early morning prayer meetings have been an integral part of spiritual discipline in Korean churches. When we trace the early morning prayer movement in Korean church history, we find that the movement was an excellent model of the accommodation principle.[21] In Korea today, almost all churches practice communal, early morning prayer meetings as part of their approach to spiritual disciplines and discipleship. This practice predates Christianity. To rise early in the morning and pray to a higher power was a generally

---

[20] For example, believing that *dwendies* (spirits) live in termite hills, some people do not remove termite hills near their house even though termites can one day damage the wooden structure of the house.

[21] The early morning prayer meetings began during the 1907 Great Awakening in Korea and were the initiative of pastor Kil Sun-Joo. See Lee Kwang Soon and Young Won Lee, *Introduction to Missiology (Seon-kyo-hak Gae-ron)* (Seoul: Presbyterian Publishing, 1993), 229.

accepted and practiced pattern in Korean spirituality. The Korean church has adopted this existing practice and utilized it in the church setting.[22]

In the Philippines, *ninong and ninang* (male and female sponsors) can be found at weddings. They promise to provide life-long counsel and wisdom to couples who are getting married. In a typical Filipino wedding, one can count several *ninongs* and *ninangs* who stand behind the couple and pledge their support. We can also ponder how such a positive cultural (contextual) category can be used in discipleship. In a similar way, festive singing and celebration are part of the Filipino social psyche. Due to the Catholic influence, Filipino people are very familiar with annual fiestas and celebrations. These are important existing categories that, when utilized properly, can help take the discipleship process one step further.

Step three: 3) create one's own discipleship material

Some discipleship materials coming from the West reflect the cultural values of individualism. For example, despite repeated emphasis on the communal aspect of discipleship in Paul's letters,[23] few topics are devoted to community life in Leroy Eims' famous book on discipleship *The Lost Art of Disciple Making*. The author presents thirty topics in the appendix under the title "Training objectives for a disciple." Of the thirty topics, only three are directly related to discipleship in community: Christian fellowship (5), love (17) and the tongue (18).[24] The other topics present discipleship as more of an individual journey with God. One of the possible reasons for this apparent lack of emphasis on community is that the discipleship movement in America was largely the work of para-church organizations (the Navigators, the Campus Crusade for Christ and so on). Moreover, Eims' book on discipleship was originally designed for use in university settings, not in local church settings where community life would be emphasized more. At any rate, such an individualistic approach to discipleship is not only unbiblical but is also alien to Asian cultures.

Creating discipleship material

Assuming that one is using other discipleship materials as a basis or a guide, there are three steps involved in creating one's own discipleship material:

---

[22] Lee, *Introduction to Missiology*, 229-230.
[23] Here are some examples of the 'one another' passages: Rom 12:10; Gal 6:2; Eph 4:32; Eph 5:19; Eph 5:21; Col 3:16; 1 Thess 5:13; 1 Thess 5:15.
[24] Leroy Eims, *The Lost Art of Disciple Making* (Grand Rapids, MI: Zondervan, 1978), 159-180.

- eliminate topics found in other materials that are not relevant in one's own context;[25]
- teach biblical themes that transcend cultures, but show how they interact with the critical issues of one's own context;[26]
- create categories not found in other contexts but which are needed in one's own context, based on the needs and issues of the local setting.[27]

Working in the Filipino context, for example, one needs to give more attention to the communal aspect of discipleship (this is a theme that transcends cultures in the Bible). However, it must be presented in the categories meaningful to the Filipino social world:

- *pakikisama* – the facility in getting along with others and maintaining a harmonious relationship
- *amor propio* – self-love in Spanish, which means self-respect; others are expected to behave in a way that avoids giving personal insult or shame (*hiya*).

Individuals and their personal space (*pagsasarili*) are important in the Philippines context. However, individuals find their identity in the group setting or in their family. In such a setting, everyone learns to value the importance of smooth relationships. Therefore, harsh and insulting words are to be avoided. An answer requiring "no" is usually softened by ambivalent phrases like "maybe…" or "it is possible…" In such a society, exposing someone to shame is the worst form of social condemnation possible.

---

[25] For example, knowledge-based, propositional truth claims are not that popular in the Philippines, much less the debate over predestination versus free will or the proof of the existence of God is hardly an issue in the Philippines context. Even those who do not come to church believe in God's existence and accept God's will. For the Filipino, what is real is not a set of doctrines but what he is able to feel. Filipino theological Jose De Mesa jokingly speaks of the Filipino "world-feel" (as opposed to "worldview"), quoting from a special lecture delivered at Asian Theological Seminary, August 15, 2003.

[26] This is perhaps the most important aspect of contextual discipleship. For this step to be effective, the person who disciples must thoroughly understand the contextual issues of the receptors. (See the chart at the end of the chapter for a sample of ideas.)

[27] For example, Bong Rin Ro proposes that evangelical contextualization of theology in Asia can 'create new categories of Asian theology according to the diversity of contexts existing in Asia. Several areas have already been suggested such as the theology of suffering and poverty, the theology of change for the Chinese according to Confucius' Book of Change, the theology of demons, and the theology of evangelism under totalitarian rule.' Ro Bong Rin, "Contextualization: Asian Theology," in *Biblical Theology in Asia*, ed. K. Gnanakan (Bangalore: Theological Book Trust, 1995), 14.

Step four: 4) determine the best pedagogical approach for the context

When we consider the fact that Christianity, by nature, is an imported religion, it is all the more imperative that a pedagogical approach familiar to the local context must be utilized. Effective contextualization involves the meshing of a foreign (Christian) meaning with a local form. Therefore, a proper contextual discipleship will result in the proper use of local forms, which are time-tested, effective pedagogical methods for the particular context.

Pedagogical methods for discipleship in the West typically include teaching (lecturing), small group Bible study, group sharing, one-on-one mentoring, short-term mission trips, and evangelistic outreaches. In non-Western settings, however, some of the above formats may not be as effective as when they are combined with symbols, ceremonies and rituals.[28] During the Holy Week in the Philippines, many Catholics engage in procession, in the re-enactment of the Passion, and some even in the actual crucifixion. Symbols and rituals come alive, leaving powerful imprints in the minds and hearts of the followers, especially the young. The evangelical insistence on the study of the Bible (the study of the Bible *alone*) as the chief vehicle for discipling new believers, is simply one-dimensional in a multi-dimensional world.

Jesus' pedagogical style

A look at Jesus' pedagogical style in Luke 14 shows his sensitivity to context and his creativity in discipling. Tension rises in the room while the Pharisees focus in on Jesus and look for a charge to bring against him. Nonetheless, Jesus begins his multi-dimensional teaching on discipleship. Here are some characteristics of his teaching:

- use of a real-life situation (not in a classroom!) – on the Sabbath day, Jesus heals a man suffering from dropsy; it is no longer a hypothetical situation in a Bible study; the situation is real and the stakes are high;
- use of high context communication – Jesus was very much aware of what was going on in the room, that the Pharisees were carefully watching Jesus and Jesus was also aware of what they were thinking; "When he noticed how the guests picked the places of honour at the table..."(v.7);
- use of concrete examples – "If one of you has a child..." (v. 5) or "When someone invites you..." (v.8);

---

[28] See A.H. Zahniser, *Symbols and Ceremony: Making Disciples Across Cultures* (Monrovia, CA: MARC), 1997. On the use of rite of passage in discipling, see Jim Courson, "Deepening the Bonds of Christian Community: Applying Rite of Passage Structure to the Discipling Process in Taiwan," *Missiology: An International Review*, 26 (3) 1998: 301-313.

- use of a story (parable) – "A certain man was preparing a great banquet…" (v.16)
- encouraging people to think for themselves – "Suppose one of you wants to build a tower…" (v.28);
- grounded in spiritual principles – "For all those who exalt themselves will be humbled, and those who humble themselves will be exalted" (v.11); "In the same way, those of you who do not give up everything you have cannot be my disciples" (v. 33);
- de-briefing and reinforcement – Jesus ensuring that the disciples understand what is really being taught here (v.25-35).

Our pedagogy must fit the context of the receptors. The approach must be natural to the receptors. For example, if people are not used to reading books, then, it would not be effective to do an intense Bible study as part of the discipling process. The right pedagogy for discipleship must touch upon all three dimensions of human learning: the cognitive, the affective and the volitional. We must ensure that a rich array of pedagogical approaches is employed including story-telling, use of symbols (e.g., foot washing) and rituals, and the more conventional small group or classroom teaching. However, the most important concept to bear in mind is that our pedagogy must fit the context of the receptors.

Discipleship in Context

Discipleship in context is a receptor-centred approach to disciple-making. It pays attention to context while being faithful to the message of the Bible that transcends cultures. It also pays attention to how the message that transcends contexts should be communicated. In this chapter, I have argued that it is inappropriate to borrow discipleship materials from one context and use them in another context without making due adjustments. It is inappropriate because issues in one context are different from those of another context. By ignoring this difference, the discipler conveniently avoids the issues that must be dealt with, the issues that stand in the way of the believer's maturity in Christ.

I have given, as an example, the problem of corruption in the Philippines. Discipleship in context does not give us the liberty to conceal the problem of corruption in such a context. A serious follower of Jesus Christ cannot turn a blind eye to the structural evil of corruption and injustice. If a self-professing disciple of Christ is as much part of the evil structures as an unbeliever is, then the church is in no spiritual shape to announce the reign of God to the unbelieving world. Therefore, every sincere disciple of Jesus Christ ought to ask, "How can I stay pure from the temptation of corruption?" and "What can I do to cleanse this society from the stain of corruption?" Discipleship in context calls for an astute examination of the needs and issues of the context, in light of the message of the Bible, which transcends contexts.

Questions For Reflection/Discussion

1. According to the author, what's the connection between "worldview" and discipleship? How do "needs and issues" in a culture relate to an understanding of discipleship? How does a theme like 'corruption' in the Philippines illustrate the challenges of discipleship?
2. How would Song's six "essential biblical themes" apply to your context? What are the issues that stand in the way of "making a clean break with the past" in your own context?
3. What is the significance of the example showing the contrast between individualism and community? How does this illustrate the point about "contextual discipleship materials"?
4. What are the limitations of certain formats of discipleship training? What other formats and settings does the author suggest?

The Message Which Transcends Cultures and the Contextual Issues in the Philippines: A Summary

Categories	*(Biblical) Truths which transcends contexts*	*Contextual Issues (in the Philippines setting)*
Experiencing God	God is near. He loves us. We can experience Him. God is also just. There will be punishment for the wicked.	How do Filipinos view God (also gods and spirits)? How does the Filipino understanding of the spirit world and the use of *swerte* (fate) and *bahala na* ("come what may") fare with the biblical understanding of God?
Salvation in Jesus Christ	We are utterly sinful before God. Christ died for us. We are redeemed from this sinful life when we put our trust in the *finished* work of Christ on the cross.	How do Filipinos understand the term "sin"? Who is Jesus Christ? How do the existing concepts of Christ in the Philippines (such as the *Santo Ninyo* or the *Black Nazarene*) hamper our proper understanding of Christ? How does biblical teaching compare with folk Catholic beliefs about "salvation"? What about "works"?
Living a holy life	We are called to live a holy life. The Holy Spirit helps us to lead a holy life. Prayer brings power to our life	How do I handle lust and greed? How do I control my tongue and my heart? How do people experience spiritual power?
Fellowshipping with other believers	Jesus calls us to be part of his Body. We are to love and serve one another.	What is the typical understanding of 'church' for those who come from the background of the Catholic Church? How do we love one another when we are in such dire need of resources? How do we love one another when we are so divided along socio-economic lines?
Bearing a witness in the world	God calls us to be the salt and light of the world. We need to bear the image of God, who loves justice and mercy (Micah 5:2ff.). We are also called to bring Good News to all peoples.	How do we live as God's witness in this world? What can I do to make this world a better place to live in? How should Christians approach the problems of *lusot*, *lakad*, and *lagay*? How do we share the gospel message with our neighbours from different backgrounds?
Following Jesus and making disciples	Jesus calls us to follow him faithfully. We are also to make disciples of all nations.	What does a mature disciple look like in the Philippine setting? In the urban poor setting? What are the preferred ways of teaching discipleship concepts in Filipino?

CONTEXTUALIZATION AND CHURCH LIFE

Melville Szto

Melville Szto examines how culture shapes various aspects of church life in Japan. Key events like conversion, baptism, the Lord's supper and church membership are discussed in terms of their impact on both new Christians and their extended families. The pressures of culture on Christian life (at an individual level) and on church leadership (at a communal level) are examined with reference to Japanese life, in a way that clearly brings out tensions and complexities. The author concludes with his own practical response to those issues, drawing on three decades of experience working in Japanese culture.

The issue that concerns us in this chapter is how Christian believers express their faith in authentic ways, in their own cultural contexts, as members of the local church.[1] The author has been involved for more than 30 years with Japanese Christians and Japanese churches, and it has been a great encouragement to see the way in which the church in Japan has been changing over the last few decades. However, there are a number of issues that need to be worked through in a church which receives significant input from Christian workers from other parts of Asia and from around the world. If Japanese Christians are to be truly rooted in a church which reflects Japanese culture, there are a number of matters that merit attention. The key issues that we will explore have to do with the process of Christian faith, the sequence of events that people from a culture like Japan follow when they come to Christian faith: we will consider how they embrace Christian faith, and how they connect to key elements of Christian experience like baptism and the Lord's supper. We will also consider how they live out this faith beyond the church in Japanese culture (with its very distinctive patterns), in terms of witness and service and the connections that they need to make with the community outside the church. Finally, we will consider how churches can express various aspects of their organization and character in ways that follow Japanese cultural patterns.

---

[1] Practical, but theologically informed, discussions of church can be found in J. Stott, *The Living Church* (Leicester: IVP, 2007 and Craig. Van Gelder, *The Essence of the Church: A Community Created by the Spirit* (Grand Rapids, MI: Baker, 2000).

Church Life – From Conversion to Baptism to the Lord's Supper

David Hesselgrave, who has worked in Japan and has written influential books on the church and culture,[2] has indicated the different responses that occur when people are confronted with the gospel for the first time in a culture where Christian faith is uncommon. A genuine experience of conversion would mean a discarding of the old (the former belief system) and an acceptance of the new (the Christian gospel). However, it is also possible to accept the new without rejecting the old which gives rise to *syncretism*, or to reject the old without accepting the new which results in *secularism*. True conversion will be seen in a changed life, a desire to obey Christ and to be identified with Christians, but this change does not always occur instantly. There is a process involved which makes follow-up and discipling critical for integrating new believers into the local church.

The role of baptism

It is probably true, not just in Japan, but throughout Asia, that the rite of baptism is seen as the point of departure, the point of radical break with the old in order to embrace the new. It is also usually the point of entry into the local church, even though the experience of conversion (a genuine embrace of Christian faith) may have begun earlier. As a result, in the Japanese context, any discussion of conversion and coming to faith needs to be connected to a discussion of baptism.

It is the author's experience that opposition to the faith of the Japanese believer often begins at the point where the believer seeks baptism. In short, the Japanese community sees this rite, whatever else it may not see, as the real point of departure for the would-be convert. Some Christian theologians have wondered whether there are ways to integrate or harmonize this rite of Christian initiation with comparable rites of passage within the Japanese culture as an act of contextualization. However, the recognition of baptism as a critical turning-point in religious experience, would tend to suggest that rather than attempt creating comparable rites of passage, there is a unique message communicated by the act of baptism which serves the gospel, and which should therefore not be minimized.[3]

---

[2] David J. Hesselgrave, *Planting Churches Cross-Culturally: North America and Beyond* (2nd ed.) (Grand Rapids: Baker Academic, 2000). Other recent treatments of church-planting with a similar concern for cross-cultural dimensions include J.D. Payne, *Discovering Church Planting: An Introduction to the Whats, Whys, and Hows of Global Church Planting*. Downers Grove (IL): IVP, 2009 and also Craig Ott and G. Wilson, *Global Church Planting: Biblical Principles and Best Practices for Multiplication (*Grand Rapids (MI): Baker, 2011).

[3] The mode of baptism, whether sprinkling, immersion or pouring, probably does not play such a major role so much as the actual act of baptism and all it means. However, there may be good reasons for preferring one mode over another depending on specific cultural and historical factors for a given church context.

In Japan, it appears often to be the case that an initial profession of faith does not necessarily lead to baptism and the individual concerned joining a local church. So much seems to depend on the willingness of the believer or would-be believer to make a decisive break, in religious terms, with family or society that is closely associated with the act of baptism. This raises the issue of whether such a break should be emphasized or whether ways should be found to create bridges between the new believer and the community, without diminishing the importance of baptism. It seems that there are two sets of issues to be addressed: the need to minimize the distancing of the new believer from the Japanese community (without a loss of Christian identity) and the need to work out how to create a sequence of Christian initiation and framework that leads to a genuine embrace of faith without the loss of the individual from the Japanese community.

The timing of baptism and the Lord's supper

Any discussion of the relationship between conversion and baptism gives rise to the question of the proper time for a new believer to be baptized. Given that relatively few people in Japan are Christians and that people who become Christians do so as individuals who, though connected to their extended families, tend to be distanced from them through moving towards Christian faith there are sometimes good reasons for delaying baptism. There is one particular denomination, in Japan, that spreads the discipleship process over three stages: 1) when a person became a Christian they were allowed to participate in the Lord's Supper; 2) baptism is the second stage and is preceded by thorough instruction regarding the significance and meaning of baptism and the role of the Christian in church and community; 3) the third stage, not concurrent with baptism, is church membership, and this is again preceded by instruction on all that was involved in being a member of that particular church.

There are, of course, occasions where there are good reasons for delaying baptism. A spouse may feel it right to wait for an opposing husband or wife to come to faith or at least to accept their partner's new beliefs, or a child might need to wait for their parents' permission. From the church's side, there may also be the need to observe over a period of time to see whether conversion has been genuine. There are people who profess faith for wrong motives. On the other hand there are also those who want to avoid baptism because of the personal cost involved.

When we were planting our first church, in the city of Tomakomai in Hokkaido,[4] we wanted to begin celebrating the Lord's Supper after our first baptism. At that time, besides the newly baptized young man, there were

---

[4] Melville Szto, *Where Your Treasure Is* (Singapore: Genesis Books, Armour Publishing, 2003), 104.

two others attending our little church who had been baptised in other churches. We had three people who were clearly identified as believers with whom we could begin. However, there were also others who had believed, but who were not baptised, and for two ladies, at least, this was not from *not* wanting to be baptised, but because of opposition from their husbands. We had counselled them to wait a while for baptism. We had to decide what we would do. There were questions that we had to address. Should the Lord's Supper be given only to those who had been baptised? Should we allow others to participate as well? In the final analysis, the Lord's Supper was a remembrance meal of Christ's work on the cross for our salvation, and intended for all who had experienced that salvation. I remember agonising over this matter, consulting commentaries and books about theology to seek understanding for a cultural context where other factors seemed to come into play.

Questions about Baptism, the Lord's Supper and Membership for the Church in Japan

1. Does discipling take place before baptism or after, or both before and after?
2. Should baptism and church membership be concurrent, or should they be separate events?
3. What are some of the reasons why a believer might choose to delay baptism for a period of time?
4. Are there biblical considerations for requiring a person to be first baptized before taking the Lord's Supper?
5. At what point might a believer who has made a profession of faith take part in the Lord's Supper?
6. On what basis does a person become a member of a local church?

It was the normal practice of the group of churches we worked with, the Evangelical Churches Association, to allow only those who were baptised to take part in the Lord's Supper, but I could not find direct support for this position from the Scriptures. The problem never seemed to arise in the New Testament because generally those who believed were baptised immediately. As a result, there were probably some people baptised who may not have had a genuine or very deep experience of Christian faith, like Simon the magician in Acts 8 (see vs. 13, 20-23). This could well have contributed to the later practice in the church of requiring catechism before baptism. In the end, we decided to allow those who had clearly embraced Christian faith and wanted to be baptised, but who had to delay a while (for practical reasons), to take part in the Lord's Supper. (Later, after around one year, to conform to the practice of our other churches, we changed this practice – during that year, however, a few believers who were not yet baptized actually participated in the Lord's Supper, held on the first Sunday of each month.)

One Sunday, I was surprised when one of our seekers told me after the church service that she had believed that very morning, and what was more, had immediately taken part in the Lord's Supper.[5] It was, according to her, the words of Scripture read during the Communion service, and not the content of my sermon that morning, that had brought her to a point where she wanted to embrace Christian faith. Paul declared that whenever we celebrate the Lord's Supper we proclaim the Lord's death until He returns, and it was wonderful to see someone actually brought to faith through this proclamation of the gospel through the Lord's Supper. This lady did, in fact, proceed to be baptized in due course. Reflecting on these matters from the point of view of the scriptures and Japanese culture, it is clear that both baptism and the Lord's Supper are urged in Scripture, but the question of the sequence in which they come is not necessarily so straightforward an issue to decide.

Church Life and Christian Witness Beyond the Church

We have considered the issues of baptism, the Lord's supper and the timings involved in the different steps of the process of coming to faith in Japanese culture. Now, we also need to look at the role and impact of local Christians in their homes and communities. One of the immediate challenges facing a new believer is how they relate as a Christian to their family, friends and work. Every culture and society has its own unwritten rules, and expectations of its members. The new Christian will need to circumnavigate these – at times to declare their inability as a Christian to perform certain duties, at other times, to change the manner of their participation in community activities.

Christian witness in the home and community

In Japanese culture, local communities set aside times when community members are expected to participate in cleaning their immediate environment, picking up rubbish, cleaning up public areas near their home and so on. The problem, for Christians, is that these activities almost always occur on Sunday mornings. Christians need to decide how they are going to handle this in a way that reflects their commitment to the community as well as to the church. They can sacrifice going to church on the Sunday morning, or they can choose to go a little later after completing a suitable portion of the work. Some believers choose to work at a different time, say the Saturday before, but of course this means not working

---

[5] Szto, *Where Your Treasure Is,* 107.

together with neighbours, and so missing an opportunity for building relationships with the local community.

Christians in Japan face an even bigger challenge from the expectation that one should conform to what one's group does. This "group" can be the family, the extended family, or the company for which one works. For example, new employees are expected to join their supervisor and other workers to go drinking after the work day. Drinking in Japan is the time-honoured means of getting rid of the stresses of the day, and also a time for building trust and good relationships. Many a new Christian, freshly graduated from high school or university and newly entered into the workforce, stumbles at this challenge to faith. Scripture does not condemn drinking *per se*, but it does speak about the dangers connected to excessive drinking. The problem is that employees do not just drink as a social exercise: to foster the building of deeper ties of trust and friendship, they are often expected to drink to the point of inebriation. Many new Christian employees find taking a stand too costly and compromise. Here again, the "quality" of a person's conversion is the determining factor in the person's willingness to take the risk of being seen as "disloyal" or a "misfit" because of their greater loyalty to Christ.

Such dilemmas raise a number of very practical questions: Christians need to consider how they honour God and yet be viable witnesses in their community, when involvement with church can cut them off from meaningful contact with their community; they need to think about how they can be witnesses in their work-places without alienating their fellow-workers by their non-participation in activities that they (as Christians) feel would not honour the God in whom they have put their trust.[6] These issues are particularly acute in a culture like Japan, where there are relatively few Christians and where becoming a Christian and adopting a distinctive Christian lifestyle can often seem to cut off people from the communities.[7] Sometimes, responses to these dilemmas can come more easily to one outside the culture than someone living within the culture. A genuine faith, peace with God, love for people, and joy in work are qualities that will, in time, become visible to the people around, but without a strong faith and sense of awe and gratitude for what Christ has done, it is all too easy to compromise. It is even possible to hide the fact that one is a Christian, in order not to become, "the nail that sticks out that gets hammered down" as

---

[6] A recent summary of challenges for the church in Asia, as it bears witness in society, from the writings of Bishop Hwa Yung, can be found in Warren R. Beattie, "Learning Lessons from an Asian Church Leader," In *Global Mission: Reflections and Case studies in Contextualization for the Whole Church,* ed. by Rose Dowsett (Pasadena, CA: William Carey Library 2011), 85-96.

[7] The issue of how to develop a distinctive Christian lifestyle and the challenges of this in Asia are clearly shared in Vinoth Ramachandra, *Church and Mission in the New Asia* (Singapore: CSCA, 2009).

an often quoted Japanese proverb says. The pressure to conform is very strong in Japan.

Questions About Community Participation and the Church in Japan

1. How can Christians honour God and be viable witnesses in their community when involvement with church cuts them off from much meaningful contact with their community?
2. How can they be witnesses in their work-places without alienating their fellow-workers by their non-participation in activities that they feel would not honour the God they have put their trust in?
3. How might this affect programmes, times and location of meetings so that church members can engage in community activities?

Christian witness as a theme for contextualization

These dilemmas reflect issues in contextualization because the local church in Japan – a context where the number of Christians is very small – must guard against becoming a ghetto. If it wants to be a truly contextual church, it needs to seek deliberately and consciously to be part of its immediate community and to avoid being isolated. Let me give an example of this. Grace Community Church (in Hokkaido) is seeking to link the church more closely with the community. By employing members' homes as centres for worship, fellowship and outreach they seek both to reach people in the immediate neighbourhoods of believers, as well as to encourage believers themselves to witness and exercise spiritual gifts for the building up of the church. The large church building serves not only as a venue for combined worship services and a host of other meetings, but also provides access to members of the non-Christian community to a variety of community activities, such as bazaars and festivals. The local photographic club, of which the pastor and several staff are members, are also allowed to display their photos in one part of the building, changing them at regular intervals.

It could be questioned whether this is contextualization and if it would not be more appropriate to see these approaches rather as methods of evangelistic outreach. However, one could argue that this is contextualized evangelism (or pre-evangelism), insofar as it represents an attempt to provide services that are socially and culturally appropriate to that society. [8]

---

[8] This is a common tension in Asia where the church's role in society is constantly questioned. There are churches in the author's own country of Singapore that make an effort to provide community services – medical, social, and recreational. By doing this, churches make it clear that they are willing to play a role in their communities, and this has helped to commend the gospel to society.

Christians are called to be both salt and light: they fulfil this role when they are actively and visibly part of their local communities.[9]

Christian witness and cultural rituals

During the process of discipleship, new believers will also need to learn to distinguish what are cultural elements from what are religious elements in their own societies. We believe the Holy Spirit in the heart of a true believer guides that person into all the truth, but the Spirit's guidance is usually through other Christians – the new believer needs to be taught. For example, in Japan, bowing is the usual form of greeting when people meet; it is also a way of showing respect, and it can even be an expression of worship. When people put their hands together and bow before the coffin at a funeral, it is usually an expression of worship, but it could also be simply an expression of respect for the dead person that is expected of all who attend the funeral. Christians generally see this as an aspect of ancestor worship and usually refrain from this action, but they do this at the cost of being misunderstood by family and relatives.

There are more overtly religious practices like the offering of incense, the offering of food, and speaking to the dead. The offering of flowers at Christian funeral services seems to be a contextualization of sorts, as it allows participants at the funeral to do something for the dead person that seems appropriate in this culture. The Christian interpretation of this ritual action is that the flowers are not offered to the dead person, but are used for decorating the casket or are a way to show affection for the loved one. Such distinctions, though important, are not easily decided and new believers will often find it confusing to know how to behave in a distinctively Christian manner, without proper teaching.

Some churches have replaced certain religious practices with Christian ones: the "*Shichi Go San*" ceremony (literally the "7-5-3" ceremony) when children of ages three, five or seven are taken to the local Shinto shrine to receive a blessing from the priest, can be substituted with a church ceremony whereby church members' children can be specially prayed for. Some churches do this regularly, every week, as a part of the Sunday worship service. They have a special prayer of blessing for the children who attend the service. It is important that Christian churches in countries like Japan, think about how they respond to the many cultural activities in society. They need to develop ways of responding at an individual level, and, on occasion, it can be helpful to develop alternative activities that are appropriate for Christians and yet fit in with the local culture.

---

[9] In Singapore, local festivals are also utilized by some churches to build bridges into their immediate communities.

BOOK IDEA
> Dowsett, Rose (ed). *Global Mission: Reflections and Case studies.* Pasadena,
> CA: William Carey Library, 2011.

The theme of "ministry across cultures" is at the heart of this book: it considers how to understand the bible (ch1) and read the bible (ch4) in a contextual manner; it discusses context's impact on church and pastoral life (ch9) and looks at how specific church activities such as memorial (ch14) and Christmas services (ch19) might be made "contextual" in Asian cultures. The book offers reflections on how a wide range of themes like multiculturalism (ch6), tribalism (ch7), hospitality (ch23), and music (ch24) are affected by context. Although there is a strong Asian emphasis, examples are chosen from around the world.

Church Life – Cultural Factors Affecting Ethos and Leadership

In this final section, we are going to look at contextualization and how it relates to other aspects of church life such as the ethos of the church, its organization and its leadership.

The ethos and architecture of the church

It is a curious fact, that whilst there is no intrinsic need for churches in countries like Japan, in Asia, to adopt western architectural church designs, many have chosen to do so. Anthropologists may lament the fact, but the world has grown so rapidly to become the global village that Marshall McLuhan[10] envisaged, that it probably is not such an important issue that Asian churches have not adopted more contextualized church buildings, since the major cities of Asia, including Japan, all exhibit numerous examples of western-style architecture – although there are also innovative designs that seek to emphasize the local culture. In a place like Japan, which is relatively open to outside influences, it is probably not a huge drawback that the regular external image of the church tends to follow that seen on western Christmas cards.[11] However, this may not be true in Asian countries where Christians are still a small minority in an unfriendly environment, or where the people are poor, or where Christianity is prohibited, and careful thought needs to be given to the kind of building or meeting place that would be appropriate for a local church. In some countries it would be provocative at best if not foolhardy, not to add

---

[10] Marshall Mcluhan and Quentin Fiore, *The Medium is the Massage: an Inventory of Effects* (London: Penguin Modern Classics, 2008).
[11] The author is nevertheless a little baffled that some pastors in Japan seem to feel their churches are somehow lacking if they do not possess a pipe organ – which is not in any way a typical musical instrument in Japanese culture!

questionable stewardship, to attempt to build churches following the traditional western pattern.

More pertinent, however, than the buildings the church erects, is the understanding of the nature and role of the church, and the witness of the church in the local community. In Japan, it would appear that there is need for a building of some kind (set in its own space) to communicate the fact that the church is there to stay; even small congregations try to obtain land and a building as soon as they can afford it. There are some current attempts to create "cell churches" or "house churches," but it remains to be seen how these will fare in the long run without owning property of their own. When the church has its own property and building it not only gives believers a sense of "permanency" but also gives the church visibility and opens up the way for it to play a role in the life of the wider community.

The organization of the church

Confucian societies (like China, Korea and Japan) tend to be hierarchical, and this is reflected in leadership structures within the church.[12] This provides a challenge for church-planters who desire to see lay members playing a greater role in the church rather than leaving everything to ordained or trained ministers. To be fair, this is an issue in churches in other parts of the world, and the challenge will always remain to find the right balance between inspired spiritual leadership and active lay participation in the life and witness of the local church. Especially in rural contexts where churches are small and cannot afford to pay the salary for a pastor, churches need to address how believers can be encouraged to exercise leadership while still working in secular jobs. Congregations need to consider how leaders for such churches are selected and trained and to what extent ordination is required for leadership roles to function.

Church organization and leadership in rural Japan

1. How should leaders for rural churches be selected and trained?
2. Are ordained ministers the only people who can celebrate the sacraments?
3. In what ways can rural churches function without ordained leadership?
4. In rural contexts where churches are small and cannot afford to pay the salary for a pastor, how can believers be encouraged to exercise leadership while still working in secular jobs?

---

[12] For a discussion of Asian culture and hierarchical leadership patterns see Steve Taylor, "Patron-Client Relationships: A Challenge for the Thai Church," *Mission Round Table* 3(1) 2007: 16-21.

The leadership of the church

It would seem that in the more developed Asian countries, there has been an over-dependence on western forms of theological education, and on western forms of church governing, whether Episcopal, Presbyterian or Congregational or combinations of these. In the large modern cities, where the successful churches are the ones with strong leadership and strong organizational structures, this has not been a particular problem. However, more creative thinking is needed for churches in rural settings, where pastors trained in more western (or global) settings are often not willing to go. "Theological Education by Extension" (TEE) has been used in some countries to provide theological training for local leaders who cannot afford the time or finances to go to training institutions in the cities or in other countries. There is certainly need for training in context, but one wonders if the training materials used are always adequately contextualized for the local situations and not just material imported and adapted from western-style seminary programs.[13] It can often seem that there has been an over-emphasis on the need for adequate theological training with a consequent de-emphasis on the priority of the call to service wherever God directs.

In a church-planting situation, where the norms are not already set by a denominational structure, there are numerous issues which need to be addressed and resolved. These include the following issues: the designation of leaders who are entitled to preach the word of God; the designation of leaders who are allowed to administer the sacraments; the question of whether in smaller congregations only ordained ministers can do these things or can other church leaders share in these ministries. As we look at the example of the apostle Paul, and think of the kinds of leaders that he appointed in all the fledging churches he planted, there are a number of questions that arise: – How did he select leaders? What kind of training did he give them? How was their authority recognized by the local congregations? Was the laying on of hands the equivalent of our present day exercise of ordination – or did it signify the conveying of spiritual gifts necessary to the task commissioned?

These could be described as theological questions rather than simply questions of contextualization, but they have relevance to the development of healthy, growing churches. In the context of a culture like Japan, where small churches are wrestling with finding patterns of church life and leadership that fit with the local context, they need to be discussed against the background of theological solutions that are appropriate for the special needs of the church in the context of Japan.

---

[13] For a wider discussion of the curriculum and ethos of theological education in Asia see Allan Harkness (ed.), *Tending the Seedbeds: Educational Perspectives on Theological Education in Asia.* Quezon City, Philippines: Asia Theological Association, 2010.

The identity of the church

There is a tendency to see the church in Confucian societies like Japan as a teaching institution rather than as a *community of believers* who meet regularly for worship, service and fellowship. In a teaching institution the role of the teacher (minister) is all-important. Where the emphasis is on the community of believers, however, there is greater scope for the exercise of believers' gifts and a greater role for lay leadership. Several churches in Japan are pioneering new approaches which seek to reduce the gap between clergy and laity. In one large church, which has adopted the cell-church system, the pastor is himself a member of one of the cell-churches, and everyone addresses each other by their first names rather than their surnames, including the pastor himself. What is more, they address him without using the title "sensei" (Rev.) and he is not the leader of the group to which he belongs. This is innovative and even radical for a Confucian culture like Japan. The cell-groups do meet for Sunday worship in a large central church, where this particular pastor still does most of the preaching, but cell-leaders conduct the baptisms of people who come to faith through their own cell churches. This church recently changed its name from "Teine Evangelical Christian Church" to "Grace Community" to reflect the fact that the church is composed as a composite of all the communities from the cell churches which are held in different homes.

The issue of titles for leaders is of great significance in Japan. In another church, known to the author, the pastor even encourages the young people, among whom he has a significant ministry, to call him by his first name *without* attaching "san" (Mr/Mrs/Ms) which is normally never done except by members of one's immediate family or very close friends. He does this to make the point that the church is also a family, whose members are brothers and sisters in Christ. Once again, this is contextualization that is the result of theological reflection on the nature of the church. Such contextualization is carried out not to fit in with local culture but to show how Christianity is radically different from the prevailing culture.

Further Reading on Church and Contextualization

DeYmaz, M. *Building a Healthy Multi-Ethnic Church, Mandate, Commitments, and Practices of a Diverse Congregation.* San Francisco, CA: John Wiley & Sons, 2007. (A Leadership Network Publication.)

Milne, B. *Dynamic Diversity: The New Humanity for Today and Tomorrow.* Leicester: IVP, 2006.

Ott, C. and Gene Wilson. *Global Church Planting.* Grand Rapids, MI: Baker Academic, 2011.

Roxburgh, A. *Introducing the Missional Church.* Grand Rapids, MI: Baker books, 2009.

Conclusion

As we conclude, we need to reflect about the purpose of contextualization in a culture like Japan. We need to consider whether we are simply seeking to make the gospel and the church more acceptable and less alien to the local culture by contextualizing, or whether we are seeking to establish an authentic representation of the Church, the body of Christ, in the local context. Though it may not necessarily be culturally harmonious, nevertheless, such a church has an attraction that draws people in spite of its cultural differences. We need to remember that people are more drawn by an authentic display of love and fellowship, "See, how these Christians love one another!" than by a church simply seeking to be attractive by adopting culturally contextualized (hence inoffensive) symbols and practices. Naturally, this does not have to be an either-or proposition, and there are ways to plant churches that are both authentic as well as culturally appropriate. There is a temptation to try so hard to be culturally contextualized that we forget that there is much in the gospel that is counter-cultural. It is refreshing to see Christian leaders who recognize this truth and become "pariahs" among their contemporaries (other pastors) by their willingness to embrace these counter-cultural implications of the gospel.

In this chapter, we have considered several aspects of church life. We have seen that church practices, church organization and the practical outworking of theological issues are all themes that form part of the contextualization of church life. In a culture like Japan, churches will sometimes opt for ways of doing things that are different from the prevailing culture so that they can model a distinctively Christian approach to culture. This, too, can be a form of contextualization – recognizing that churches need to be careful not to alienate themselves from local Japanese culture and that they need to build bridges to the local community as they seek to bear witness to their Christian faith.

Questions for Reflection/Discussion

1. 1. What are some of the ways in which baptism is a "decisive" event for Christians in Japanese culture?
2. What might be the advantages of the model of three stages of Christian life in Japanese culture – 1) belief; 2) baptism; and 3) church membership – where profession of faith at the first stage, is accompanied by an invitation to participate right away in the Lord's supper?
3. What are some of the challenges to discipleship of conformity in Japanese work culture?
4. What are some of the special challenges for church life and discipleship for people living in a "group culture"?

5. Given the relatively small size of the church in Japan, they face a number of issues with training, developing and deploying leaders. What are some of the lessons that we can learn from the Japanese context?

CONTEXTUALIZATION AND BIBLICAL TEACHING

David Harley

David Harley shows how different sections of the bible reflect a sensitivity to the culture of their original audience, in terms of the ideas chosen, and the way in which they are communicated. He illustrates this from the Old Testament, from the stories about Jesus recorded in the Gospels and from Paul. He encourages those who teach and preach to be sensitive, not just to culture's influence on concepts and ideas, but to the way in which the style and formats of teaching (and preaching) will influence the impact of our ideas on our hearers. Engaging in ministry across cultures, it is important to be flexible and adaptable in both our choice of teaching methods and their content.

Christians are called to preach the gospel to all the peoples of South East Asia so that by God's grace the church is established there. As an essential part of that process we are called to teach the Bible. We may be involved in teaching the Bible to one person or we may lead a small group. We may be teaching regularly in a church or we may be on the faculty of a college or seminary. During the 1990s, I lived in Singapore, where I taught at the Discipleship Training Centre, a residential training college, and subsequently at Trinity Theological College. I have also taught courses at Singapore Bible College, Malaysia Bible Seminary and Bangkok Bible College. When I became General Director of OMF International, I travelled throughout East and South East Asia. Both in my work in Singapore and my travels throughout Asia, I was constantly reminded of the need to teach appropriately depending on the context and the cultural setting.

At one level or another we are all engaged in teaching God's word and, as cross-cultural workers, we are called to do so within a culture that is usually quite different to our own. We are teaching people who may have a different worldview, who may notice things in the Bible we had never observed and who also may misunderstand many of the things they read. We all face the challenge of making God's word intelligible and relevant to those to whom we speak and at the same time remaining faithful to biblical truth.

Contextualization Starts With God

In our search for the effective communication of God's truth, the best place to start is with God himself and to examine the way in which the omniscient Creator has communicated with those whom he has created. As God made a self-revelation to the patriarchs and subsequently to their descendants, God did so within the cultural and historical framework in which they lived. Indeed, one could say that every word of divine revelation is an example whereby God, who is infinite, seeks to communicate truth to finite human beings. For example, God allows a description in anthropomorphic language so that God's people may gain some idea of what God is like. Although God is a spirit and has no body, the descriptions in the bible portray God as if God had a body, face, arms, and so on, so that God's people can relate to God as a person. God is portrayed as being sad or laughing because these are terms they can understand, even though they are inadequate to describe the one who is transcendent.

Yet, God places limits on how far the personality of God can be described in these ways. Scripture never resorts to describing God in the kind of terms that were used of the numerous deities found in Canaanite or Babylonian myths. They were often described as eating too much, getting drunk, losing their temper and making love. God uses language that the reader of the bible can understand but does not allow biblical truth to be distorted by the use of inappropriate terms or analogies. One of the most striking examples of divine contextualization in the Old Testament is found in the term that God chooses to convey the idea of special relationship between God and God's chosen people – namely the term "covenant." When God makes a covenant with Abraham in Genesis 15, God uses a ceremony with which Abraham is familiar. In this ceremony, a covenant or treaty is signed between two parties, when each party passes through the divided carcasses of sacrificed animals. The symbolism is striking and obvious. Later, when God seals the covenant with the children of Israel at Sinai, the ceremony follows a pattern of treaty signing that was familiar at that period in the ancient near east. As God seeks to communicate the special relationship of grace that has been created between God and the people of Israel, it is expressed in terms that are intelligible to them in their own cultural and historical context. God is contextualizing the message to be conveyed.

There are other examples in the Old Testament when God will *not* use language or ideas from the contemporary culture to convey what God wishes to say, if the language or ideas so used will give the wrong impression. A good example of this is found in the concept of king or *melek*. The idea of God as king is prevalent in the whole of the Old Testament and lies behind the term covenant that we have just considered. However, the specific term *melek* is not used in the early periods of Israel's history for the simple and obvious reason that the word *melek* could easily be confused with the term *molek*. *Molek* was a particularly fierce Canaanite deity who required the sacrifice of children as part of his worship. As William Dyrness writes, "Exodus 15 speaks of the Lord reigning for ever but there is some reticence to speak of God simply as king."[1] It is only later

---

[1] William Dyrness, *Themes in Old Testament Theology* (Cape Town: Oxford University Press, 1979), 47.

in the history of Israel when the danger of this confusion had subsided that we find several references to God as king or *melek*.

We have seen then that God seeks to communicate as effectively as possible to the people of God who are living within a specific historical and cultural context. God is prepared to use words that they can readily understand but is careful to restrict or limit such usage where there is a danger that truth will be distorted. This already provides us with some guidelines as we seek to communicate God's truth to people who come from different cultural backgrounds. We must use words they understand but beware of those terms that may be misunderstood or may lead to a wrong view of God. A Christian in an Islamic context once said that Christians in her country find it very hard to read the Old Testament with its constant reference to the nation of Israel. The same may well be true in Malaysia and Indonesia. One student from Indonesia recently told me that they even try to avoid using the term Israel when speaking of Jesus or the disciples. This immediately alerts us to the sensitivity we need when choosing which words to use in our teaching. It is obviously impossible in one short chapter to cover the whole of Scripture and to suggest how we might approach the teaching of each book and each literary genre. We need to be selective. As a result, we will examine the biblical prologue and the Patriarchal narratives of Genesis, before considering the examples of Jesus and Paul. We will conclude by considering the importance of the *way* we teach as well as the *content* that we communicate.

Explaining the Biblical Prologue

The prologue of Genesis sets out the foundation of the biblical world, the building blocks on which the rest of biblical teaching is erected. Here, we are presented with teaching on the essential character of God, the nature of God's created world, the nature of human beings and their relationship to God. We find God's pattern for human relationships in the context of marriage and we see the biblical analysis of what is wrong with our world. In every culture or religious worldview there is a similar series of building blocks that shape their basic understanding of the world. There is usually some understanding of God or the spirit world, some understanding of creation and the origin of mankind, and some analysis of the cause of sin and suffering. Our task as Bible teachers is to bridge the gap between the biblical worldview and that of the receptor culture. As an example, let us consider what aspects of God's character are revealed in the first two chapters of Genesis. These chapters show that God exists, that God is the creator of everything, and that God is one (though there are some hints of plurality within the Godhead). We also learn that God is powerful, wise and good, that God speaks, and reveals himself to those who have been created and enters into a personal relationship with them.

As teachers of the bible in another culture, our task is to present these basic fundamental biblical truths and to point out where they differ from the view of God or the spirit world that is found in other religions. Islam has a similar view of God, though there are significant differences. Buddhism does not believe in a personal God at all, though, in practice, prayers are given and offerings are made to the spirit world. People coming from a tribal or traditional background may have some belief in a Creator God, but are more concerned with the nature gods or ancestral spirits, who seem to be more involved in their everyday lives. Such peoples often have stories about a Creator God who used to live close to them but who has now gone away because people were so bad. The challenge we face is to understand the worldview of the group we are addressing, to note the differences between their understanding and biblical teaching, and then to build bridges that will correct their understanding and bring them to a correct understanding of God's truth.

Sadly, Christians in the past have sometimes failed to do that. They were either unaware of the worldview of their hearers or they chose not to address it. As a result, some of their converts professed faith in Jesus while retaining a worldview that was totally inconsistent with Scripture. Some converts from animism or folk Buddhism will continue to attend the temple or pray to the spirits in times of sickness or family crisis. Unless we understand and address the worldview of those we teach, those who come to faith and become baptised members of the church, may well become confused and experience a kind of spiritual schizophrenia.

Suggested Reading on Teaching Across Cultures

Lingenfelter, J. *Teaching Cross-Culturally: an Incarnational Model for Learning and Teaching.* Grand Rapids, MI: Baker, 2005.

Moreau, A. S., E. H. Campbell and S. Greener. *Effective Intercultural Communication: A Christian Perspective.* Grand Rapids, MI: Baker Academic, 2014. (Encountering Mission.)

Teaching from the Patriarchal Narratives

The patriarchal stories are largely set in rural farming communities in the ancient (Asian) near east. While the culture that they depict may seem strange to those who live in the west, it is closer to the culture of many who live in other parts of the world, especially those who live in rural communities. When people from those communities read or hear the patriarchal stories, the stories may well resonate with them and they may notice many aspects of those stories that we had never observed.

Preaching on the Old Testament and "Curses"

Once, when I was preaching in the majority world, in a Bishop's private chapel, I spoke on the call of Abraham in Genesis 12 and, as far as I was aware, I had covered satisfactorily the main points in the passage. However, the Bishop did not agree and told me that I had missed out one of the most significant points in the story – I had said nothing about curses! "Yet in our culture," he said, "we take curses very seriously. There are over two hundred references to curses in Scripture and the Bible says that Jesus has become a curse for us. When you preach in non-western cultures from a passage like this, you must talk about curses." It was an important lesson for me to realize that people from another cultural background will read things in the Bible that I, personally, may well ignore.

Dreams play a prominent part in these stories. God spoke to Abimelech, Isaac, Jacob, Joseph, Pharaoh, a butler and a baker through dreams. If we come from the west, we may not take dreams very seriously and may assume that they are the product of overwork or over-eating. People in other cultures will place far more importance on dreams and, as we address these stories, will want advice as to how they can understand their dreams and know whether or not God is speaking through them. Genealogies are found in Genesis and in many other parts of the Bible. We may wonder why they are there and may hardly ever bother to read them. We may not see the point, but many people from different backgrounds may find them to be extremely significant. I knew one Christian leader who came from a tribal background and who became a Christian simply by reading the genealogies. They proved to him the authenticity and historicity of the Bible. They showed him that the characters in the Bible, including Jesus, were real people, who had their own genealogy just as he had.

There are numerous references to sacrifice both in Genesis and throughout the Scriptures. In western secular societies, ideas of sacrifice and the shedding of blood seem strange and even repulsive. In many other cultures, such ideas are easily understood and appreciated. Most of the world religions, as they are observed by ordinary people, contain ceremonies involving sacrifice and the shedding of blood. An evangelist once told me that he always preached from Leviticus at funerals because everyone at the ceremony, Christian and non-Christian alike, could understand what he was talking about.

Our task, as those wishing to teach the word of God, is to try to read the biblical text through the eyes of those to whom we are speaking. What will they misunderstand? What will they notice? What will raise questions in their minds? What will seem most relevant to them or form a natural bridge with some practice or tradition in their own cultural background?

Learning From The Master

When we turn to the New Testament, we are at once confronted with the master communicator, Jesus Christ. He provides us with the perfect model of how to communicate effectively, whether it is to simple country folk who have little education, or to highly-educated religious leaders. So much has been written about his style of teaching that it might seem superfluous to say anything further, but this chapter would be incomplete without some reference to those characteristics of his teaching that made him such an effective communicator. Firstly, Jesus was constantly using illustrations taken from the lives and experience of the people to whom he spoke. He talked of flowers and birds, of trees and crops, of farmers and fishermen, of sheep and wolves, of life in the home and women in the kitchen. By contrast, many sermons that are preached in the west are full of carefully worked explanations of doctrine, but often lack either illustration or application. One Asian theologian, the Japanese missionary Kosuke Koyama, was determined to follow the example of Jesus by expressing his teaching through pictures taken from life in a Thai village community. His books *Three Mile an Hour God* and *Waterbuffalo Theology* speak of paddy fields, monsoon rains, croaking frogs and cock-fighting – images which peasant farmers would easily understand.

Secondly, Jesus showed an amazing ability to adapt his message to his audience. In his conversation with Nicodemus, Jesus speaks appropriately in theological terms (he talks about the kingdom of God, cleansing with water, and the work of the Spirit of God) and refers Nicodemus back to the Old Testament Scriptures. "You are Israel's teacher and do you not understand these things?" When he addresses the Samaritan woman, he talks about finding water, reflecting the mundane task that occupies a significant part of her daily life. In both cases, he is preaching the gospel. In both cases, he is offering eternal life. In both cases he calls for a response. He shows Nicodemus that he must be born again. He calls the woman to repent of her lifestyle. In essence, the message is the same, but the way it is presented is completely different.

Thirdly, Jesus made constant use of stories. Matthew goes so far as to say that Jesus never taught anything without using a story (Matt 13:34). Jesus was well aware of the power of stories both because they catch people's attention and because they are easily remembered.

The power of stories

I remember one church where I preached a series of three expository sermons on Romans 9-11. I thought I had done a reasonable job in expounding those difficult chapters, but those sermons were quickly forgotten... On another occasion, in the same church, I preached a simple sermon based on the book *The Very Worried Sparrow* (a book based on

Matt 10:29).[2] I just told the story and made some brief application to people of different ages. Years afterwards, people still remembered the story of the sparrow. I have no doubt that we would be far more effective Bible teachers, both at home and as cross-cultural teachers of the Word, if we made more use of stories (both biblical stories and stories from beyond the bible).

Fourthly, Jesus made people think – he did not spell everything out. One of the reasons why he spoke in parables was to make his hearers reflect on the implications of what he was saying. The parable of the Prodigal Son is a good example (Luke 15:11-32). We never hear the end of the story. We are left with a number of questions still unresolved. Did the older brother listen to the father? Did he come to the party? Was he reconciled to his younger brother? Did they then divide what was left of the inheritance? Jesus leaves those questions unanswered precisely because he wanted his audience to see themselves in the story and to decide for themselves how they would respond to God's gracious invitation both to them and to those they might regard as sinners.

In our preaching, we may be guilty of the common mistake of being too precise, too dogmatic. We may want to cross every "t" and dot every "i." We want to explain every detail so that there is nothing left for our hearers to think about. We encourage people to become passive, because we tell them everything and they do not need to work things out for themselves. They are not growing to maturity. They are not learning to feed themselves from the Word of God. They are becoming the passive receptors of the truth we teach. Such an approach does not stimulate spiritual growth. Certainly there were times when Jesus proclaimed statements of absolute truth, but there were many times when he left his hearers with a question rather than a statement, when he wanted them to think, to reflect and to respond.

BOOK IDEA

> Dillon, Christine. *Telling the Gospel Through Story: Evangelism That Keeps Hearers Wanting More.* Leicester: IVP, 2012.

Stories have a real power to communicate: narrative is an important genre in the bible and "story" is an important vehicle for sharing the gospel. This book looks at the practicalities of telling stories, using the bible in groups, and using stories to connect to those beyond the church. The author works in Asia as a church-planter amongst marginalized groups; she brings a knowledge of Asian culture to this material and has developed her capacity to use stories in a cross-cultural context. She shows how important it is to share the good news of the bible's message in a way that is accessible to hearers.

---

[2] Meryl Doney, *The Very Worried Sparrow* (Oxford: Lion Hudson, 2009).

Learning From Paul – The Contextual Theologian

Paul was not a systematic theologian. Nowhere does he set out to provide a comprehensive systematic summary of Christian doctrine. It is more correct to refer to him as a pastoral or contextual theologian. Dean Flemming points out how interpreters of Paul have described him as "… a pastoral theologian, a task theologian, a missionary theologian, a hermeneutical theologian, and the like."[3] It is clear that Paul's concern was to apply gospel truth to the situations faced by the young churches. His desire was for the gospel to bear fruit in people's lives as they came to faith in Christ and grew in holiness. His letters were an extension of his missionary activity.

Paul was flexible, not in his understanding of the core of the gospel, but in his application of the gospel in each context. In each of his letters he responds to the pastoral needs of his recipients. In Galatia, Paul was concerned to combat the dangers of legalism and to demonstrate how Christ's death has delivered us from slavery to the law. In his letters to the Thessalonians, he seeks to correct wrong ideas about the second coming and urges the need for personal sanctification. In Ephesians and Colossians, his focus is on reconciliation and power. In Philippians, his emphasis is on the joy of knowing Christ and being with him for ever. In each case, Paul refers to the cross of Christ, because the cross lies at the heart of the gospel message, but his concern is to bring the implications of the death of Christ to bear in each context. So as we engage in our task of communicating gospel truth in differing cultural contexts, we need to observe both what Paul taught and how he models the application of that truth in each situation.

Paul was not inconsistent. He did not change his fundamental message. He was sensitive to his audience but he was not dictated to by his audience. He was contextual but he was not changeable.[4] At the heart of all that he taught, lay the gospel of the death and resurrection of his Lord and Saviour. For Paul, however, that gospel was like a multifaceted diamond and at any one time he would focus on one facet of gospel truth: Christ died for our sins; he set us free from the law; he set us free from the power of evil spirits; he overcame death; he gives us identity; he reconciles us to each other; he gives us purpose; he makes us children of God; he gives us abundant life; he gives us eternal life, and so on.

Our task, as we engage in cross-cultural ministry, is to proclaim the fullness of the truth of the gospel, but if we are to follow Paul's example, we shall take care to consider which aspects of Christ's salvation find immediate resonance with the people among whom we are ministering. We will not come with a rigid, one size fits all, approach. We will not start in

---

[3] Dean Flemming, *Contextualization in the New Testament* (Downers Grove, IL: Inter Varsity Press, 2005), 89.
[4] Flemming, *Contextualization in the New Testament*, 116.

the same place that we might in our own country. We may find that the use of "the four spiritual laws" is not at all helpful. For Muslim women in South East Asia, the good news is that Christ by his death enables them to have dignity as daughters of God. For those who live under constant fear of spirits and the powers of darkness, the good news is that Christ by his death has overcome all the powers and authorities of this world.

It is equally important to observe the huge range of illustrations that Paul uses to help his readers understand more fully the significance of Christ's sacrifice on the cross. He is just as much at home in using pictures from the secular contemporary world as from the Old Testament Scriptures. He draws his illustrations from the market, the school, the home, the athletics track, the law court, the building site, the garden yard, the human body, the temple. He even uses a term like *musterion* – with its dubious association to the mystery religions – and adapts it to declare the secret that God has now revealed to the world.

If we are going to follow in the footsteps of the apostle, we need to take two key lessons on board. Firstly, we need to search the Scriptures to familiarise ourselves with the plethora of pictures that are used to describe what Christ has done for us on the cross. We need to dig deep in the quarry of God's Word until we find those terms and illustrations that strike at the heart of the people whom we are seeking to build up in the faith. Secondly, we need to familiarise ourselves with the stories, histories, proverbs and customs of each people group until we find redemptive analogies that will deepen their understanding of what Christ has done for them.

Finding the Right Methodology

One of the challenges we face as we attempt to teach or preach Scripture in a cross-cultural environment is to find the right pedagogical methodology. Our teaching method may be just as important as our content. We need to avoid being too rigid and monochrome in the way we teach. Certainly the prophets in the Old Testament were extremely creative in their desire to communicate God's truth to the people of their day. They preached, they sang songs, they shared their testimonies, they enacted their message, they made puns, they used dramatic headlines and so on.[5] As someone has observed, they did not even have a piece of chalk, but they were determined that people would listen to what they had to say. We would do well to emulate their passion and to seek to be as creative and varied as possible in our style of communication.

In every culture there are traditional patterns of teaching and learning. One educational method may work well in one context but not in another. Judith Lingenfelter shares her own disastrous experience of trying to teach

---

[5] These examples are dawn from Isaiah 1, Ezekiel 32, Amos 7, Ezekiel 12, Micah 1:10 and Isaiah 5.

African-Americans in the same way that she had successfully taught in a predominantly Caucasian, middle class school.[6] She writes:

> The students did not respond as I had anticipated, they did not take tests well, some were several years below their grade level and they challenged me at every turn. I was miserable!"

When her husband chose to undertake his doctoral field work in the Pacific island of Yap, she accepted a position in an elementary school to teach a class of twenty-four children who came from six different nationalities. The experience totally changed her understanding of teaching.[7]

> Students helped one another with everything and almost never worked alone. They were personally self-sufficient, yet they tended to answer questions as a group. The five American students in the class were routinely frustrated because things were not done "right." On the playground, the island students picked lice out of one another's hair, which the American students considered "gross." In the classroom, the American students raised their hands to answer questions, which the Yapese students thought was silly.

When we teach the Bible in a cross-cultural environment, we must not assume that our students, be they children or adults, will learn or behave in the way we anticipate. We may find that the context requires us to be more informal. We may discover that dialogue, discussions, role-plays are both possible and effective. On the other hand, in South East Asian cultures, we may discover that we are expected to be more formal in the way we teach. In societies that are strongly influenced by Confucian thinking, the authority of the teacher may be paramount: their word may not be questioned. Dialogue or discussion may not be acceptable. I well remember the confusion I caused when I asked one class to discuss the morality of God hardening Pharaoh's heart. Clearly, many in the class were shocked to be asked to discuss and even more shocked to be asked to consider whether or not God was being fair.

Much has been written about the differences between western and Asian ways of thinking. Bruce Nicholls described the method of traditional western scholars as involving "abstract linear thinking, rational language and copious footnotes." He compared this to a Chinese way of thinking which he described as "thinking concretely, practically, using symbols, analogies and stories."[8] This is an important distinction and those of us who are teaching the Bible in an Asian context, especially in rural areas and among less educated people, need to ask whether the way we teach or preach is less effective simply because our method of communication is too

---

[6] Judith Lingenfelter, *Teaching Cross-Culturally* (Grand Rapids, MI: Baker, 2003), 13.

[7] Lingenfelter, *Teaching Cross-Culturally,* 14.

[8] Bruce J. Nicholls, "Contextualization in Chinese Culture" *Evangelical Review of Theology* 19 (4) 1995: 368-380.

Western. In a theological journal, the following questions were once asked by an Asian teacher: "Is straight line thinking the only way to do theology or does this linear approach sometimes lead to a truncated form of biblical understanding? How important is the story, the parable, the mystical experience or the emotional response in understanding the truth of the Bible?"[9]

Further Reading on Contextualization and Asian cultures

Adeney, B. *Strange Virtues: Ethics in a Multicultural World.* Downers Grove, IL: Intervarsity Press, 1995.

Cook, M., R. Haskell, R. Julian and Natee Tanchanpongs. *Local Theology for the Global Church.* Pasadena, CA: William Carey Library 2010.

Chan, S. *Grassroots Asian Theology: Thinking the Faith from the Ground Up.* Downers Grove, IL: IVP Academic, 2014

Yung, Hwa. *Mangoes or Bananas: the Quest for an Authentic Asian Christian Theology.* Oxford: Regnum, 1997.

While it is true that Asian Christians who have higher education may appreciate the expository sermon that is favoured in the west, with a clear and logical explanation of the text, those who come from a rural background may struggle with this kind of preaching and may prefer sermons that abound with stories and application. As Dr Albert Ting, the current principal of Singapore Bible College, once explained to me: "The country folk will not appreciate doctrinal sermons that are full of long and involved explanations. They want to know how it applies to their life and how they are to live."

Conclusion

God is the author of truth and has provided us with a model of how to communicate truth within a particular historical and cultural setting, and with illustrations that people can understand. We also observed that there are many details in the Patriarchal narratives that will resonate in many cultures in the non-western world, such as dreams, genealogies, practices of sacrifice, the significance of curses and so on, that will create natural bridges with our receptor audience. We have stressed the importance of finding appropriate cultural ways of communication rather than simply replicating the way we might teach at home. We have pointed out that people from another culture do not necessarily teach or learn in the same way that we do. It is not just *what* we communicate but *how* we

---

[9] P. Chang, "Steak, Potatoes, Peas and Chopsuey: Linear and Non-linear Thinking in Theological
Education," *Evangelical Review of Theology* 5(2) 1981: 279-286.

communicate that may make our teaching of the Bible relevant, intelligible and life-changing.

Questions for Reflection/Discussion

1. How does the author suggest that concepts used in the Old Testament like "covenant" and "king" show a sensitivity to their cultures?
2. How do the examples of curses, dreams and genealogies illustrate the idea of contextualization as "looking through the eyes of our hearers"?
3. The author shows four modes of teaching by Jesus? How might these be applied in your culture?
4. "If we are to follow Paul's example, we shall take care to consider which aspects of Christ's salvation find... resonance with the people among whom we are ministering." How might this apply to your culture?

PART THREE

EQUIPPING FOR MINISTRY

EQUIPPING LOCAL LEADERS TO CONTEXTUALIZE

Brian Michell

Brian Michell examines a vital aspect of contextualisation facing church-planters in a different culture: the way in which local leaders can be trained to lead the church into the future, ensuring a smooth transition of leadership to local people who themselves are sensitive to issues of contextualization. Drawing from his experience in Borneo, East Malaysia, he gives practical examples about seeking and developing the right people and facilitating the transition to local leaders. The author also deals with the practical issues of preparing local leaders to assume leadership and the contextual issues that they face in relation to church life and polity. The chapter ends with thoughts on how to help leaders "take definite steps to formulate and implement theologically and contextually helpful courses of action for the true welfare and witness of the church."

A vital part of the church planter's strategy to enable the development of a truly local church is the need to train suitable local leaders to lead appropriately in their context. Such a process will lead to a smooth transition of leadership from those from outside a culture to the new local leaders. In this chapter we will explore these issues in relation to the context of East Malaysia. The author, who worked in the island of Borneo in East Malaysia, was active at a crucial stage in the transition from a mission-founded church to an independent and contextual local church. The Borneo Evangelical Mission (BEM) had partnered with the China Inland Mission Overseas Missionary Fellowship from the 1950s onwards. Plans had been made to move towards an autonomous local church and with the independence of Malaya[1] in 1963, these assumed a new urgency. There was a pressing need to help produce leaders who would not only lead the local churches but who would play an increasing role in the nurture of theological education for the church.

Good entry and exit strategies are important and wise parts of effective church planting work: both involve sensitive contextualization.[2] The challenge of contextualizing the gospel is double-edged. By the grace of God and the work of the Holy Spirit, the unchanging gospel message needs to be expressed and applied in appropriate, relevant and clear ways to facilitate its reception by people living in a particular context. That same gospel will then influence and even challenge the cultural context as the

---

[1] Independence was accompanied by a change of name from Malaya to Malaysia.

[2] For a summary article on this transition see Brian J. Michell, "Leadership Development and Transition in Missionary Partnership and Closure: Observations from the OMF/Borneo Evangelical Mission (BEM) Experience in East Malaysia," *Mission Round Table* 3(1) 2007: 2-8.

word of God is accepted and applied. This progression calls for the full interplay of spiritual sensitivity, theological depth, cultural understanding and wise expression not only on the part of church planters from outside a culture, but in increasing measure from the new leaders in the emerging church.

A failure to develop suitable local leaders results in a church dominated by people and perspectives from outside the local culture. A failure to establish local leaders in a culture risks the development of a church which is perceived as exotic and foreign, irrelevant or even contrary to the character of the local community. Leaders who are weak in their understanding of the gospel and who sacrifice biblical truth for the sake of indiscriminate cultural relevance move too easily towards religious syncretism or a Christianity which embodies many aspects of the previous or prevailing religion. Leaders who are weak in their understanding of culture and who sacrifice cultural relevance for the sake of preferred foreign church norms move too easily into cultural rigidity leading to a church that is disengaged from its local context. In establishing local churches which are fully biblical and yet culturally relevant, church planters face the need to add a fourth element namely "self-theologizing" to the traditional three-self model (self-governing, self-supporting and self-propagating) and way of thinking about contextual churches.[3] The idea of thinking theologically from within the cultural environment and applying biblical truth to local situations is increasingly recognized as fundamental to the development of a fully contextual church which is relevant in its surrounding community.

The Role of Cross-Cultural Mentors

Cross-cultural mentors have a primary role in the process of preparing local leaders who will not only be well equipped to lead biblically, spiritually and organizationally, but who are also enabled to appreciate the issues and lead the church contextually and theologically. In the first instance, this calls for commitment to identify the leaders the Holy Spirit gives to his emerging church.

Seeking and Accepting Local Leaders

As in so many aspects of church planting, faith and works combine in this task of developing local leaders. "Faith" in God, demonstrated through energetic prayer that he will provide the necessary gifts to his church, and

---

[3] See Hiebert's discussion of the "three selves" from enduring ideas promoted by R. Anderson and H. Venn in the 1860s and the role of self-theologizing in relation to these concepts. Paul Hiebert, *Anthropological Insights for Missionaries*. (Grand Rapids, MI: Baker, 1985), 193-207.

'works' as the Christian worker seeks, encourages and challenges people with the perceived potential to lead well. We may (and should) pray for and seek future leaders of ability and suitability, faith and maturity, dedication and willingness, but we also need the "eyes of faith" to identify the leaders God is providing who are emerging as available and developing. We need to accept, appreciate and work with the leaders that God provides and recognize that God, as potter, moulds the lives of those in emerging churches in the same way as he moulds our own lives – in both cases working with earthen vessels shaped from the same clay. One of the challenges in selecting suitable potential leaders is that expanding local and national churches require a considerable number to fill the diverse roles at various levels. In the context of East Malaysia, specialist leaders have been needed, for theological education and pastoral training, for outreach and evangelism, for specialist ministries to children, youth, women, for meeting social needs, and for administration. The people we see and train in early years may well be in the process of being prepared by God for specialist leadership roles in later years. Our task, under God, is therefore to seek, discern, mobilize and mentor as many potential leaders as possible, both men and women, and to develop lay ministry leaders as well as those entering financially-supported church ministry. This selection process already has its contextual implications. Issues such as age and seniority, ethnic grouping, social position in the community, and the role and status of single or married women in leadership are not only theological and spiritual but also social and cultural.

Leaders Choosing Local Models of Evangelism

I remember the struggles of the SIB (the Evangelical Church of Borneo) Sarawak council in responding to the question of evangelism amongst the distinctive cultural setting of the Iban peoples. The council had been urged to allow evangelism amongst the Iban to be conducted as a recognizably Iban venture which would lead to contextualized Iban churches with their own distinctive characteristics, language, culture and leaders. Rather than requiring Iban converts to conform to the patterns, language and sub-culture of the Bahasa-Malaysia speaking SIB churches, they were to be free to follow their own cultural norms. This decision was made knowing that a growth of Iban churches and their leaders would present major challenges to the traditional leadership roles of the Council and its members.

The expatriate church planter may unwittingly import their own cultural expectations and prejudices. Alternatively, they may encounter local cultural assumptions and preferences which either complicate and hinder or facilitate and promote the work of God in the direction and growth of the church and the choice and preparation of future leaders. Again, a wise understanding of God's word and biblical models is essential, as is an associated sensitivity to local cultural norms, strengths and weaknesses.

BOOK IDEA

Plueddemann, James E. *Leading Across Cultures: Effective Ministry and Mission in the Global Church.* Downers Grove, IL: IVP Academic 2009.

The modern world with its multicultural interactions is creating new and pressing demands for leaders. Those involved in ministry face the same challenges, and this book looks at the way in which culture shapes a number of key areas of life relevant to leadership such as ambiguity, power and the interplay between the group ("collectivist" cultures) and the individual. The author looks at the human, psychological and theological aspects of leadership and brings to bear a wealth of personal experience as he advises leaders how to respond in different situations.

Training and Trusting Local Leaders

As part of the church planter's strategy to move to closure and transition, they should constantly be aware of contextualization when training local leaders, preparing them to lead relevantly as local people from a recognized Christian community working within a specific cultural environment. As training can be both formal and informal, the mentor needs to model appropriate lifestyles and attitudes – a willingness to demonstrate humility and servant leadership is crucial. Since these latter characteristics may not be highly valued in the local cultural context, Christian contextualization will involve wise understanding of biblical values and priorities and of their application in what are sometimes unsympathetic environments. Consistent and loving mentoring has the potential to shape the attitudes and expectations of future leaders who will learn more from what they see than from what they hear. I have often noted the value of good "in-service training" before a person undertakes formal theological education. Formal teaching and good academic standards are important in grounding and developing capable, mature leaders of initiative and wisdom, but they are best built on a strong foundation of guidance and discipleship from mentors in person.

In an extension of the same principle, my recommendation is always for primary ministry and theological training to be conducted in the local cultural context and only subsequently for trainees to go elsewhere for advanced training if necessary. Initial grounding and shaping are highly influential, and training within the local culture establishes patterns of contextually-relevant ministry and leadership of lifelong value, especially in such areas as communication and teaching, attitudes and relationships, economics and lifestyle. Such patterns of leadership will subsequently be modelled by those local leaders as they care for the local, regional or national church and its witness within that cultural context. Again, it is vital to think about appropriate contextual training early on as part of a strategy that looks to the future of the church and to a transition to local leaders. A church planter who wants to train local leaders who are contextually sensitive and relevant, as well as biblically and theologically mature, needs to think about the bigger picture of the church's overall leadership and not just about individual leaders. Church polity and the structures of leadership for groups of churches should be filtered and influenced by the same criteria and goals of being contextually appropriate.

The principles of contextual sensitivity apply equally to the timing and formulation of church polity – the legal and practical framework of how church life is conducted. It should avoid two extremes: 1) pre-packaged models from another culture which are imposed too early; 2) models that leave too many options vague, open and uncertain, which results in confusion, conflict or even competition between emerging leaders. Ideally, emerging leaders from within the culture should have a significant role to play in shaping structures, associations and patterns of operation of the emerging church. Whether formal or informal, good training involves delegation and the opportunity for practice, and these in turn require wise and gracious guidance and supervision. As the SIB denomination grew in the late 1970s and 1980s, they had to deal with the implementation of new patterns of church government and structure. As the variety of ethnic groups diversified, more details needed to be clarified concerning the structures and systems for the benefit and harmony of all. The goal in transition should be to train future leaders who are wise and sensitive about contextualization and who will, in turn, produce like-minded leaders – this requires mentors who already practise contextualization with a degree of perception about their own efforts at church planting!

Transition to partnership with local leaders

The dynamics of a church planter's relationship with an emerging church and its leaders change as the work progresses. As described in the classic[4] four stages of transition, the relationship should move from "Pioneer" through "Mentor" to "Partner" and ultimately to "Participant." As people believe, and as a new church develops, the initial pioneering role moves more towards the nurturing and discipling functions of a mentor. Then, the relationship shifts increasingly into a partnership mode, which encourages developing leaders to exercise responsible use of their gifts: appropriate support, respect and space must be accorded to them for this to happen. A good partnership phase facilitates the establishment of strong and wise leadership and ultimately an autonomous local programme in which others from outside may subsequently bring helpful contribution as participants within that contextually-oriented programme.

---

[4] Terms used by Harold Fuller (slightly adapted) in a well-known study of the transition from "mission to church." Harold Fuller, *Church-Mission Dynamics* (Pasadena, CA: William Carey Library, 1980).

All partnerships require commitment to cooperation and mutual support, agreed goals and methods, and sensitivity in relationships and expression. Cross-cultural partnerships demand even more in their need to understand the cultural and contextual factors present. Wise practice by the church planter in this area will not only help with developing relationships and with the church, but will also provide useful insights and models for the future attitudes and activities of an emerging leader. [5] Some areas of this cross-cultural interface which may need particular sensitivity and wisdom include: authority structures and decision-making processes; age and gender issues; women's ministry and leadership; the handling of finances, reporting and accountability; ethnicity and status in the wider community; formally-appointed leadership and voluntary lay leadership.

Preparing Local Leaders to Assume Leadership

Strong entrepreneurial mission partners who plant churches may well have the gifts and drive to establish and lead a new church, but such character strengths do not guarantee sensitivity and self-restraint. The commitment to so develop competent contextualizing local leaders and to transfer leadership opportunity and responsibility to them thus needs to be conscious and consistent on the part of the missionary. Self-restraint will be required on the part of the missionary whose head is full of ideas and whose heart is full of concern that all will be done rightly and well under God.

Leadership in the longhouse

If we are to train local leaders to think and lead biblically and contextually, we need to do more than simply teach and guide, model and pray; we must also be willing to hold back and give emerging leaders the opportunity and responsibility to reflect, decide and act on their own. If we do not do this, we run the risk either of never letting go and allowing local leaders to lead, or of their ultimately coming to the stage of reflection, decision and action only after we have departed without the possibility of discussion and support during the transitional phase. In the latter stages of national church leadership development, I have frequently felt that some of my most strategic times of help and training took place sitting on the floor of a longhouse or in a pastor's home late at night after meetings were finished and I was just talking together with national colleagues. This was not a time for laying down the law on issues or courses of action, but rather a space to share together on ideas and issues. It allowed principles about doctrinal or

---

[5] For a recent insightful discussion of cross-cultural partnerships and finance, see Mary T. Lederleitner, *Cross-Cultural Partnerships – Navigating the Complexities of Money and Mission* (Downers Grove, IL: Inter Varsity Press, 2010).

organizational matters to be raised and led to reflection on courses of action that could be developed regarding pastoral concerns. I have had the opportunity to share biblical or pastoral pointers and then open up the potential implications of these – and then leave the leaders to reflect, make their own responsible decisions, and put them into action.

The sociological dimensions of the cultural context will also need to be evaluated. How are leaders regarded? What is the self-perception and sense of identity of the leader? How far do leadership values of popularity, power, and prestige influence the church and its emerging local leaders, and how do they cope with such expectations or temptations? Missional models of unity and harmony, humility and cooperation will have a powerful influence. Our burden and prayer here is to so teach and model so that Scripture and culture are brought together clearly and constructively in the hearts, minds and lives of the growing leaders. One of the major issues in preparing locals for autonomous leadership is the question of salary level and the source of financial support. As the "golden rule" has it, "whoever pays the gold sets the rules!" [6] External financial support of local pastors and leaders may seem an effective fast track to development, but it commonly leads to continuing dependence and external control which militates against true contextualization of and by local leaders. In East Malaysia, we practised a policy of no financial support for local church workers, (though some limited support through the church was directed to primary evangelists). In a review of this policy and the wider church's development ten years after the withdrawal of Christian workers from outside, the unanimous assessment of church leaders was that this practice "was a good policy" and "because of this… [the church] is now strong and self-supporting." [7]

Phasing out cross-cultural mentors

It is not always easy to know when and how to let go of leadership and when a trainee leader is ready to take over, especially when, as a mentor and trainer, the church planter has become very close to the emerging leader having travelled so much of the path of discipleship together. Steffen maintains that closure strategies should be formulated even before the church-planting process begins [8] but it is not necessarily possible to tie such phasing out and withdrawal measures to a particular timeframe as situations and responses vary widely.

[6] This is a phrase used in Latin America – with a certain degree of irony – but highlighting a real and sensitive issue.
[7] Brian Michell, "The Role of Missionary Partnership and Closure in Indigenous Church Development." Unpublished Doctor of Missiology Thesis, Asian Graduate School of Theology, Manila, the Philippines, 2004, 218.
[8] Tom Steffen, *Passing the Baton: Church Planting That Empowers* (Rev.Ed.) (La Habra, CA: Centre for Organization and Ministry Development, 1997), 5-8.

Nevertheless, the wise church planter has clear goals in view for the anticipated stages of growth in the church and the development of leaders and ministries. These stages become part of the framework for contextualized leadership and would include the following: meeting in a systematic way together with leaders for worship, teaching and fellowship; helping leaders develop specific ministries as needed and suitable in the context; creating leadership structures and training for emerging leaders; helping with the nurture, training and discipleship of believers; showing leaders how to accept responsibility for financial support and pastoral care; passing on the ongoing work of evangelism and outreach; discussing how to reflect and apply God's word in the context in which the emerging church is located. As particular forms of expression or activity in these areas are delineated, they can be identified as scheduled stages and related to timetabled milestones in planning or review. Without them, it becomes too easy for the development of local leadership to drift or to be perpetually postponed. If one of the goals of church planting is to see the emergence of a theologically mature leadership which is capable of contextualizing, then this too needs to be consciously scheduled into the church planter's teaching and mentoring programme in both informal and formal training. Having done their part in teaching and developing, the church planter then needs to be prepared to trust the Holy Spirit to guide and work. The fruit of the Spirit in self-control applies here in a willingness to hold back and give new leaders room to exercise their leadership, even to make mistakes, and pray they will learn from those mistakes. In the final analysis, it is Christ's church not the Christian worker's church, and we are to cultivate the church's dependence on him as Lord and Master.

The concept of progressive withdrawal is a practical and helpful approach in this interactive process of closure. It applies to how leaders share in committees as well. There should be a conscious attempt to relinquish participation. This involves a conscious movement from being leader of a committee, then reducing to being an active member, then reducing further to a limited participation and ultimately resignation from the committee. Such a process is both feasible and wise. A similar movement of withdrawal applies to sharing ideas in an informal way – this can take place in the context of meetings and later with the leader outside the committee forum (when asked for such help). Such input can shape and support the leader's and committee's thinking and expectations for a limited period – recognizing that even indirect involvement sustained too long runs into the danger of continuing to drive the operation from behind the scenes. Once a colleague who was pastoring a growing town church

communicated these back to the younger pastor. In the process, the particular church received help, the church pastor and leaders learned to look to their own national leadership, the president and central executive were extended in their understanding and strengthened in their leadership, and they were equipped to cope with the issue when it arose again in a different situation. In addition, the colleague learned to work with direction from national leadership.

If our goal as cross-cultural workers is simply to lead the new emerging church, we may well just continue leading. We need to recognize, however, that no matter how well we lead, we will still be leading as outsiders to the culture. [9] If our goal is to develop mature competent local leaders who can work biblically and spiritually through issues and lead in their own contexts, then our practice should and ought to be oriented consciously in that direction – and lead ultimately to a specific point of transition of leadership and a phasing out of outside Christian workers. If we have done our part, then we can and should trust God to lead his people in their ongoing witness, ministry and leadership in the local context.

The Role Of Local Leaders

As already highlighted, the training of local leaders who can and will contextualize with theological wisdom, cultural sensitivity and spiritual vitality involves a fully co-operating partnership between the church planter and the emerging local leader, as both walk in step with the Holy Spirit. This equipping depends initially on the understanding, commitment and effort of the church planter. It also depends ultimately on the insight, willingness and action of the leader being trained. This latter process in turn brings together the biblical depth and spiritual growth of the local leader and their understanding of the cultural context, plus their perceptive application of the word of God guided by the Holy Spirit to that context at all levels and in all relationships and activities. Much here depends on the effort and action of the leader who is called and trained.

Identifying the role of local people as leaders

The expectations of an emerging Christian community and the norms practised in their context may both help and hinder the exercise of contextualized biblical leadership. The practice of political or community leadership may carry patterns of behaviour and underlying attitudes at variance with biblical teaching and standards.[10] A Christian leader needs to

---

[9] For cooperation with leaders from different cultures see James E. Plueddemann, *Leading Across Cultures: Effective Ministry and Mission in the Global Church* (Downers Grove, IL: IVP Academic, 2009).

[10] See for example Matt 20: 25-28.

be able to evaluate their own context as a prior step to applying biblical principles to the conduct of leadership within that context. A rejection of the Christian framework risks leadership styles being less than truly biblical and a neglect of the cultural framework risks leaders who are not truly contextual in their example and influence. A leader who aims to contextualize the gospel in their own context needs to study to understand the nature, role and goals of a contextualized church in that context, so that believers in turn will be taught and enabled to be still true to their culture and context while fully true to their Lord and Saviour. The old adage, "One more Christian, one less Chinese" refers to the fact that to become a Christian meant to abandon one's cultural identity. This tragically reflects the failure to contextualize the gospel and church not just in China, but also in the contexts of Chinese diaspora cultures like Malaysia.

Ultimately, it is the biblical revelation and the Holy Spirit's guidance which should primarily shape the expression of the gospel and the character of the church in a particular context. The varieties of Christian experience from different historical periods, and from different places, will help in shaping the church's expression in any given context, as will the experiences of a church planter who founds a church. (The latter should not become determinative for the contextualizing leader.) It is helpful if the new leaders can be encouraged to see themselves as an interpreter *between* cultural contexts as well as an analyst of their *own* context and a developer of a culturally-appropriate, biblical church within that context. Some aspects of the local culture and context may need particular exposure to the searchlight of God's Word in this process of biblical contextualization by local leaders. This may include the benefits and obligations of leadership such as status and privilege, confidential pastoral information, and the expectations of a leader's extended family and friends for benefits which may follow from the leader's access to church resources and finance.

Suggested Reading on Leadership Across Cultures

Branson, M. L. and J. F. Martinez. *Church, Cultures and Leadership: a Practical Theology of Congregations and Ethnicities.* Downers Grove, IL: IVP Academic, 2011.

Elmer, D. *Cross-cultural Conflict: Building Relationships for Effective Ministry.* Downers Grove, IL: IVP Academic, 1993.

Lederleitner, M. T. *Cross-Cultural Partnerships – Navigating the Complexities of Money and Mission.* Downers Grove, IL: Inter Varsity Press, 2010.

Handling social and national contexts

The contextualizing leader not only works with the source material of the biblical context and other cultures, but also with the various levels of society within the home culture. Local leaders – especially those active at a regional or national level – need to apply universal requirements of leadership in the particular contexts of their ministry. These will include some of the following: how to express in relevant and appropriate ways clear and resolute opinions about vision and direction; how to guard against internal politics in the church; how to deal with ethnic, regional, urban or rural favouritism in church decisions and actions; how to develop an ability to cope with differences of opinion; how to have courage to "grasp the nettle" of difficult situations and to work graciously towards just and righteous problem resolution. As the church developed nationally, the Combined Executive of the SIB Sabah, SIB Sarawak and the BEM established a Cultural Affairs committee to consider issues of contextualization.

Leaders giving advice on daily life

The committee researched a number of issues which member and leaders faced in their daily lives. They wanted to be able to clarify what it meant to contextualize the gospel within the local ethnic groups and cultures. Guidance was given to the churches on the following matters: feasts and food at weddings; customs and practices on the occasion of births; engagements; marriages and deaths; initiation into adulthood and inheritance rights; bride price; justice and retribution; adoption; divorce and remarriage; and the consequences of former slavery. This was a clear example of the local church becoming a self-theologizing church.[11]

There is also the need for wisdom to handle continuing relationships with present and former mission partners, historically connected mission organizations, and other outside church groups both within the country and from overseas. Wisdom, strength and grace may be needed to maintain and develop friendships and partnerships at appropriate levels, especially when aspects of indigenous church autonomy and external influence or financial assistance are involved. Local views on doctrine or church polity may also be areas that face challenge from such external influences. A further issue in the concentric circles of connections is that of relating to the wider community, the nation and the wider world, so that the ongoing task of contextualization will be applied not only in the traditional cultural context but also in a rapidly changing contemporary world. Secular materialism, religious pluralism, extremism, the dominance of major world religions, ethnic and racial issues and tensions, regional and national politics, and the national government's expectations and requirements will all call for clear recognition of the issues: they also require biblical and wise responses by

---

[11] See the records of the 1980s: SIB (the Evangelical Church of Borneo), The Minutes of the combined SIB Sabah & Sarawak Komiti Adat-Istiadat (the Evangelical Church of Borneo), Unpublished Minutes, held by the SIB Church, Sabah, East Malaysia.

the church leader who is committed to contextually-sensitive Christian
leadership.

Thinking through complex issues

Many of the above aspects of church, community or national life will not
be easy for new leaders to cope with, especially if those leaders are still
growing in theological maturity and contextual understanding. It may well
be in this situation that experienced partners from other cultures can have a
particularly helpful contribution in highlighting issues and bringing
relevant biblical principles into the discussion as local leaders explore and
evaluate their context. Similarly, emerging church leaders can be helpfully
encouraged to create and use good working relationships with other
national churches and church associations. Some of the issues to be worked
through by emerging contextualizing leaders arise from international links,
with former mission partners or missionary organizations, and with other
church groups who wish to enter into partnership with the emerging church,
perhaps through contact with members studying, working or travelling
abroad. Sometimes, such groups may prove to be strongly directive in their
influence and assistance, and can push the emerging church to comply with
their own frameworks. Here, in particular, the contextually-sensitive leader
of the emerging church will need the perception, strength and willingness
to think through developments and implications and accept only input that
is helpful and healthy for the local church. Wise partnerships from former
mission partners and local colleagues can be of significant help.

Another area of international and local church sensitivity for the
developing leadership of the national church is that of financial assistance
and the associated expectations of the donors. Some donors come with a
desire to take over the church and claim it as theirs. Others wish to redirect
and reshape it. Still others may be happy with the character and ministry of
the church but wish to be very directive in determining how their gifts
should be used. Most will have expectations of efficient and prompt use of
donated funds with full and transparent reporting and accountability. The
challenges of accounting and book-keeping procedures and requirements of
high standards of administration can also raise significant problems for
churches working within their own cultural context yet required to straddle
cultures in these matters.[12]

Implementing contextualized courses of action

Having recognized contextual issues and worked through the cultural and
biblical implications, leaders then need to take definite steps to formulate
and implement theologically and contextually helpful courses of action for

---

[12] See Lederleitner, *Cross-Cultural Partnerships* for guidelines in this area.

the true welfare and witness of the church. Continuing biblical teaching and theological training are increasingly important for leaders who are concerned to develop the work of contextualizing the church. As missionary church planters and teachers withdraw, this need may become more pressing. Well-trained locals and selected specialist teachers, as participants in the church's theology-training programmes, will play a crucial part at this stage – and the lack of suitably and sufficiently prepared local leaders at this level will be very costly for the church's long-term life and direction.

At one stage in Sarawak, the state government enacted legislation affirming various traditional cultural practices as the official law for all members of the designated ethnic groups. Since many of these practices originated from primal religious roots and had spirit-worshipping associations, this raised major concerns in the church. The Evangelical Church in association with mission leaders then established a Cultural Affairs Committee to investigate what elements of the cultural traditions of its varied ethnic member groups were universally characteristic of those groups, and what elements were associated with previous religion and biblically unacceptable for Christians. Proposals were formulated concerning cultural traditions and practices which applied to all members of the respective ethnic groups and could acceptably be applied to Christians of those groups, while aspects which were counter to Christian belief and practice were excluded. Representations were then made to government and accepted. Had this not been done, legal matters such as inheritance, marriage, funerals, land ownership, would have seriously disadvantaged Christians or compromised Christian standards. The Committee eventually delivered recommendations[13] on a wide range of contextual cultural issues which eliminated possible stumbling blocks for current and potential Christians.

Conclusion

The challenge continues for leaders with the perception, ability and will to contextualize the gospel and church in their own communities. Styles of leadership, processes of decision-making and communication, the expression and application of the gospel in church and society, forms and expressions of spirituality, ways and means of effective teaching and training, administrative methods and processes, ethical standards and behaviour, handling of finances and material resources, theological formulations and applications, and the development of church polity will all continue to need and benefit from thoughtful, biblical and sensitive contextualizing by leaders in emerging and growing national churches.

---

[13] SIB, The Minutes of the combined SIB.

Questions for Reflection/Discussion

1. What are some key of the formal and informal situations in which a church-planter can mentor local leaders – modelling appropriate, biblical lifestyles and attitudes?

2. If you are in partnership with local leaders, how can you exercise wisdom and sensitivity in the following areas: "authority structures and decision-making processes"; "age and gender issues"; "women's ministry and leadership"; "handling of finances, reporting and accountability"; "ethnicity and status in the wider community"; "formally-appointed leadership and voluntary lay leadership"?

3. How can individual local leaders in your midst be encouraged to see themselves as "interpreters of cultural contexts," "analysts of their own contexts" and "developers of a culturally-appropriate, biblical church within their own contexts?"

CREATING A COMMUNITY
FOR CONTEXTUAL LEARNING

Warren R. Beattie

Warren R. Beattie aims to help those involved in training and theological education to apply contextual thinking to teaching. Using the model of the multicultural community of the Discipleship Training Centre, in Singapore, he shows how one theological institution has adopted contextual approaches to teaching, learning, worship and other aspects of its community life. The chapter also considers the importance of relationships, approaches to mentoring, ways of preserving Asian cultural sensitivities and how to connect the curriculum to Asian themes and concerns.

In a review of theological education at the end of the 20th century, Robert Banks suggests that missional centres have been at the forefront of creative approaches to theological education.[1] This chapter will show how one such centre with a missional[2] identity – the Discipleship Training Centre (DTC) in Singapore – has adopted a model of education that offers effective training for ministry, for students who come from a number of cultures in Asia.[3]

Introducing the DTC Community

DTC is based in Singapore and it offers theological education in a residential setting tucked away in the suburbs near the busy commercial centre of the city. Singapore itself is a Pacific-rim city that celebrates diversity and issues of multiculturalism are commonly discussed in the local media. Although the majority of Singaporeans are ethnically Chinese (around 70%) and Mandarin is commonly used in society, English is designated as the "work language": signs on the island often include

---

[1] The author has found the following book especially relevant for contextual learning communities who want to explore creative approaches to theological education – Robert Banks, *Re-envisioning Theological Education: Exploring a Missional Alternative to Current Models* (Grand Rapids, MI: Eerdmans, 2000).

[2] DTC is not strictly a mission training centre but mission studies have been at the heart of the community since its inception; staff have included colleagues like David Adeney, Howard Peskett and David Harley (amongst others) who have published in the area of Mission Studies and been involved in mission training in a wide variety of cultural contexts.

[3] The approach of a residential-based learning community that takes seriously its identity as a community and which puts a high value on character also addresses many of the issued faced by theological educators in terms of the ministry / academic balance.

English, Mandarin, Malay and Tamil scripts to represent the languages of the four main people groups on the island. It is to this social context that DTC invites students – who are already graduates in other disciplines – for a two-year long theological programme which offers training for ministry.[4] In recent years, the community has numbered some twelve to twenty students with four or five core staff. The core staff team lives on-site as part of the community and its numbers are supplemented by adjunct lecturers who come in to teach each semester.[5] Countries represented have routinely included Singapore, Malaysia, Indonesia, Thailand, Hong Kong, Korea, Japan, Pakistan and India (mainly North-East states or Tamil Nadu). Occasionally, students have come from places like Burma-Myanmar, Cambodia or Vietnam or from further afield. They represent churches from "mainline" denominations (including the Church of South India, and the Mar Thoma church) and other independent Protestant churches.

The whole of DTC life revolves around the community and the relationships that exist between staff and students who see themselves as disciples of Christ Jesus on a journey of faith – living, studying, teaching and interacting together. The community itself is shaped by its residential character, based in an old-fashioned building surrounded by palms and shrubs in this quintessential garden city. The weekly timetable of academic learning is punctuated by daily chapels and small group times in college and in the homes of lecturers during the weekends. On Sundays, the community disperses to various churches in Singapore where staff and members are involved in ministry and as part of the larger body of Christ in the city. It is in this community setting, in a cosmopolitan and modern city in multicultural South East Asia, that DTC offers theological education and training for a multicultural community drawn from across Asia. The limitations of a traditional western theological education for non-western peoples are commonly acknowledged to be a source of grievance by theologians in the majority world. The Sri Lankan theologian Sugirtharajah[6] speaks of his sense of the loss of his Asian heritage, exchanged for "a mess of theological pottage" provided by his education in the west. John Mbiti, describes his confusion and consternation when, on his return to Africa from a centre of theological excellence in Germany, confronted with an apparent case of possession, he felt a real gap between his western theological training and the pastoral demands of the African

---

[4] In recent years they have added the option of doing a one-year version of the course in Intercultural Studies.
[5] Staff have come from Singapore, Malaysia, the Asian diaspora in Australia and elsewhere, from the West especially the U.K. (occasionally from North America) and from other Asian countries like the Philippines and Indonesia.
[6] See the introduction to R.S. Sugirtharajah (ed.) *Frontiers in Asian Christian Theology: Emerging Trends* (N.Y.: Orbis, 1994).

context.[7] In what follows, we will explore some of the ways in which DTC tries to overcome these limitations for Asian students in its learning community and environment.

We should note that the concept of "discipleship" at the heart of the DTC community's outlook, which could be seen as promoting a model of theological education that focuses purely on the practical aspects, can be a more all-embracing approach to ministry.[8] The Canadian theologian Hall, suggests that more attention should be given to "how theological education... can illumine and facilitate a contemporary form of discipleship." As a result, "rather than concentrating on *the inner life of the believer*, this orients it to, and contextualizes it in, the here and now of daily life in the service of the kingdom..."[9] In this regard, the DTC model does two things: 1) it connects an understanding of discipleship to the whole setting of the community, embracing the communal, personal and academic elements of the training; 2) it also acknowledges that, in the New Testament, Jesus' own relationship with his disciples models the idea that he chose disciples "that they might be with him and that he might send them out to preach..." (Mark 3:14) Such a model recognizes that there are academic aspects of discipleship, in terms of developing a biblical world-view, and being able to apply biblical thinking rigorously and strenuously to every area of life and ministry. The interest in the New Testament of going to "make disciples of all nations..." (Matt 28:19) reminds us that discipleship is not to be an inward directed attitude, rather it looks outwards to the whole world with its different cultural communities and nations.

A Multicultural Community and Contextual Learning

The idea of a multicultural community which engages in ministry and uses its own diversity as a starting-point is not new. As the New Testament describes in Acts, the world of the early church included a diverse world of peoples and identities. The people with whom the apostle Paul worked – Paul's missionary band or team and his "colleagues" – were drawn from different parts of the Mediterranean. Banks suggests that such diversity can be used positively when it comes to modern contexts and for theological education in particular: "A more effective strategy calls for a team of

---

[7] John Mbiti,"Theological Impotence and the Universality of the Church," In *Mission Trends No 3: Third World Theologies,* ed. by G.H. Anderson and T. E. Stransky, 6-18 (New York: Paulist Press & Grand Rapids, MI: Eerdmans, 1976).

[8] For a stretching theological exploration of discipleship see David Bosch, *Transforming Mission*, Maryknoll: Orbis, 1991.

[9] Halls is quoted in Banks, *Re-envisioning Theological Education,* 162-163. Banks notices that as a result such an approach "would require us to focus less on how to integrate spiritual formation (using the language of spiritual disciplines) into theological education."

people that reflects the pluralistic nature of those they are seeking to serve in the world. Paul's diverse band of co-workers is an excellent model."[10]

Multicultural communities that look outwards

A survey of the New Testament reminds us that all discussions about the diverse nature of the church are firmly and inescapably rooted in specific historical and geographical settings. As the New Testament shows in Acts, the world of the early church included a diverse world of peoples and identities. Michael Green has pointed out that the ethnic and cultural character of the early church was more varied than we often imagine.[11] He illustrates his point from the likely origins and cultural leanings of members of the church in Antioch, as described in Acts 13 – Lucius is from Cyrene (in North Africa); Simeon, "called Niger," presumably comes from a black African culture; and Manaen's education and proximity to the royal family links him to the cultured world of the Mediterranean elites. The church universal is well-placed to challenge its own traditions of mono-cultural models of education – but it needs to be willing to do so. "Having incorporated a variety of cultural groups into its history and tradition, the church possesses global voices that can offer the cultural knowledge theological education needs in order to break with its ethnocentrism."[12] Theological educators are beginning to do this, reflecting on these issues in different centres. A recent, serious discussion of multicultural theological education from the United States,[13] shows an understandable preoccupation with three ethnic groups of special relevance to the contemporary church in the United States.[14] In a similar way, a book on theological education in

---

[10] Banks, *Re-envisioning Theological Education,* 130-135. Banks further sees the advantage of "the missional model of theological education" which "places the main emphasis on theological mission, on hands-on partnership in ministry", which learning takes place in "actual service" and "obedience," allowing due place for reflection on practice, 135-148.

[11] Michael Green, *Acts for Today* (London: Hodder and Stoughton, 1993), 122-123.

[12] See Jose R. Irizarry, "Toward an intercultural approach to theological education for ministry," in *Shaping Beloved Community,* 37.

[13] The discussion is also shaped by issues such as 'multiculturalism,' 'diversity,' 'gender,'and 'difference' that would resonate with the modern context of the United States and its social debates. This is not to suggest that the book does not address the agenda of 'multiculturalism' and so on in a critical way – in fact it addresses these issues – but the discussion is clearly shaped by the North American context and certain cultures. See David V. Esterline and Ogbu U. Kalu (eds.), *Shaping Beloved Community: Multicultural Theological Education* (Louisville, KY: Westminster/John Knox Press, 2006).

[14] The ethnic groups are Hispanics, Black Americans and Asians (in particular, Koreans). Multicultural diversity is given careful scrutiny and Hiebert concludes that, "The real knowledge we gained was that valuing diversity does not consist of an "anything goes" attitude; it consists, rather of a willingness to engage in a

Asia makes much of its Asian setting: it refers to Asian peoples; the Asian context and its realities; and the "Asian mind."[15] Contextual learning communities must be sensitive to issues of culture, but they must connect them to their own specific geographical settings and to the ethnic groups which are based there.

In a multicultural learning community, the task of contextualizing learning for students from different cultures has several dimensions. The community itself needs to provide an environment, which is welcoming and appropriate for people from a range of cultures, in its everyday life as well as inside the classroom. As a learning community it should prepare students who are able to contextualize Christian faith, mission, church life and discipleship when they return to their own (or other) cultures.[16]

Developing inter-personal skills in a learning community

Community is also a good setting for developing inter-personal skills. The most highly valued characteristics in cross-cultural workers are "empathy and flexibility."[17] David Harley, who has been Dean of two very different multicultural centres of theological education, describes the need for those involved in cross-cultural work to be "ethno-radiant." These qualities cannot be developed in isolation from interactions with a wide range of people, and a learning community made up of members from different cultures provides an excellent context for developing such skills.[18]

---

respectful process of mutual transformation that can happen only with those who are from worlds entirely not our own." Theodore Hiebert et al, "The Tower of Babel and Cultural Diversity: A Case Study on Engaging Diversity in the Classroom," in *Shaping Beloved Community*, 128-141.

[15] Larry W. Caldwell, "How Asian is Asian Theological Education?" in *Tending the Seedbeds: Educational Perspectives on Theological Education in Asia,* ed. by Allan Harkness (Quezon City, Philippines: Asia Theological Association, 2010), 32-33; other authors explore characteristics of the "Asian mind" – and the differences between attention and control, between relationships and categories, see Perry W. H. Shaw, "'New treasures with the Old': Addressing Culture and Gender Imperialism in Higher Level Theological Education." in *Tending the Seedbeds*, 50ff.

[16] In this regard, a commitment to a missional stance – a willingness to look outwards in service can be a useful part of the formation.

[17] For a fuller discussion on member care and mission in Asia, see Stroma Beattie, "Enhancing Member Care in the Singapore Context: Towards Good Practice and the Resolution of Problematic Issues," in *Missions Matrix: Navigating 21st Century Missiological Issues,* ed. by Florence Tan, 103-133. (Singapore: Singapore Bible College, 2009).

[18] Many practical issues for a contextual learning community, especially the qualities required for staff and students, are explored in David Harley, *Preparing to Serve (*Pasadena, CA: William Carey Library, 1995).

Staff should be able to model these qualities: the experience of DTC bears out the recently expressed desire that the faculty in theological centres represent different cultures so that learning communities can be more sensitive to the issues of cross-cultural learning. Communal life and outside ministry experiences are needed to give staff and students opportunities to work together in multicultural teams[19] which model the diversity of the wider Christian community.[20]

Relational Aspects of a Contextual Learning Community

The ability to "get on" with people is a desirable quality in many cultures and this is especially true in Asia, where cultures are highly relational and "group-centred." The DTC community's experience of ministry is based around relationships with people of other cultures, developed in the context of residential-based community.

The relational aspects of community in Asian contexts

It is easy to talk in general terms about the importance of relationships, and about the teacher as mentor, but we need to take account of specific cultural realities in Asia. Asian cultures can put a certain premium on the category of "teacher" – in Korean there is a proverb that says, "One should not even step on a teacher's shadow." Asian words for "teacher" are often used as a title of respect which are applied more widely to people who are "honoured": this is true, for example, of the Korean term for teacher "*sŏnsĕng*" and the Japanese word "*sensei*." Students from cultures like these, may hold certain expectations about the role of teachers and students (even post-graduate students) which will need to be addressed in a contextual learning community. Both a sense of hierarchy, and terms of respect, are deep-rooted in Asian cultures. In the Singaporean context, titles are often added to people's names in local languages. Some terms like "Uncle" or "Auntie," for those who are significantly older, transfer easily into English. Terms like Doctor, Pastor, Reverend are common, but are

---

[19] This is not to say that the "benefits" of "multiculturalism" should be uncritically accepted without appropriate critique: Esterline and Kalu show that intercultural education can mean learning from "sharing the same space" not simply that you add many different ideas together. See David V. Esterline, "Multicultural theological education and leadership for a church without walls," in *Shaping Beloved Community,* 15-27 and Ogbu U. Kalu, "Multicultural theological education in a non-western context: Africa, 1975-2000, in *Shaping Beloved Community* 225-242. We need to recognize also that the various cultural expressions of multiculturalism are often different – the dominant ethnic groups differ considerably in places like Singapore, Malaysia, Australia and the U.S.A.

[20] See Banks *Re-envisioning Theological Education,* 149ff., for more information on this topic.

sometimes used with the first name to reflect greater informality: hence Dr. Helen, Reverend Timothy, and Pastor Graham; Elder as a title, as in "Elder Derek" (for church elders), which is common in Singapore, would seem more awkward to English speakers outside of Asia.

Asian patterns of relating

A notional framework or hierarchy of relationships extends well beyond teachers or older people. In Korean, there are different words for boys and girls to use of older brothers *hyŏng* (or *o-ppa* for girls) and older sisters *nun-na* (or *ŏn-ni* for girls) and other Asian cultures have similar usages, reflecting how deeply ingrained is the impulse to classify relationships in Asian societies. "Brother" and "sister," in this sense can extend to friends and classmates, and woe betide the younger person who uses a friend's first name rather than the appropriate title. In educational contexts in Korea, "*sŏn-bĕ*" is used for "classmate in the class above" both as a designation and a "title"; the equivalent for the class below is "*hu-bĕ*." These terms function in Korean (and other Asian languages) *instead* of names and can carry with them many cultural expectations or obligations. Despite post-modern preoccupations about equality, the only "flat structures" in Asian cultures are squashed cardboard boxes about to be recycled! Students from certain Asian cultures will relate to each other with these "hierarchies" and "obligations" very much in mind.

A multicultural learning community needs to find ways to resolve tensions, when English is used as a medium of education in contexts where people have very different expectations about what to call each other. Students who feel they are abandoning cultural norms too quickly in what they call others, or who are forced into alien modes of relating, will not feel at home with lecturers or with fellow students.

Relational aspects of learning

Relational ministry is a feature of the mission teams in the New Testament. Banks notes the ways in which Paul's relationship to his team shaped his teaching and equipping: the idea of "imitation-of" was applied to both Paul himself and to Christ; it also shaped his thinking about the close relationships between himself and Timothy and Epaphroditus. Those who were close to Paul were involved in daily activities with him: the purpose of these groups was to promote "active service or mission in furthering the kingdom, as initially defined by a key figure and progressively clarified by the whole group."[21]

Relational ministry also features in discussions of Asian theological education, with the book *Tending the Seedbeds* looking at the role of staff

---

[21] Banks, *Re-envisioning Theological Education,* 118, 119-120 and 123.

as mentors, as well as lecturers, in the context of "learning for ministry." In this model, staff are seen as guides and facilitators rather than simply "knowledge-dispensers." [22] This is certainly part of the DTC experience, where staff mentor and encourage (as well as model for) students in the classroom: they share by example in leading worship, participating in services, and by their contributions in ministry outside the classroom and beyond the college boundaries as well.[23] It has been suggested that "interpersonal exchanges" are at the heart of teaching and that the ability to stress local elements in teaching (rather than those that are global or universal) is facilitated by taking account of individual students, their stories and their cultures.[24] Authentic multicultural education really means creating theological education that is more genuinely human and more culturally relevant, not just promoting "diversity" for its own sake. To do this effectively means cultivating positive and meaningful relationships between staff and students, which takes account of members of the learning community as individual human beings who bring a rich heritage of personal insights and skills which are shaped by their distinctive cultural heritage and their learning environments.

Relational aspects of teaching and mentoring

All theological communities will facilitate personal interactions between staff and students. It is important that staff are allowed time to interact deeply with students as individuals, recognizing that they are shaped by their culture as well as their personalities. Such interaction will help develop and shape disciples of Christ Jesus with due regard to their cultural backgrounds and individuality that reflects the pattern of training that we see in the New Testament.

Creating contexts for mentoring

Mentoring can take place at different levels, but will involve some contact with students on a one-to-one basis, in small groups and in a variety of more ministry-specific events. Small group times allow space for staff to get to know students and for all of us to get to know one another. At DTC, weekly group meetings with students – some of which are traditional small

---

[22] David Burke, "Time to Leave the Wilderness? The Teaching of Pastoral Theology in South East Asia," In *Tending the Seedbeds,* 253.
[23] This connects to educational theories that seeing teaching involving sharing life as well as knowledge. See Banks, *Re-envisioning,* 170-175 and Ian Payne, "Reproducing Leaders Through Mentoring," In *Tending the Seedbeds,* 171-3. Interestingly, this theme also surfaces in the west in the writings of the eminent educationalist and psychologist Howard Gardner.
[24] Brawley draws on Freire. Robert L. Brawley, "Teaching the Bible in a Global Context," in *Shaping Beloved Community,* 122,

group meetings (in college or in staff homes) and some of which are more like group outings – help everyone to share more deeply about their experience of theological education. Interactions between staff and students from different cultural backgrounds allows for an extending of horizons on *both* sides. Looking at biblical themes, spirituality, church life, worship or the concerns of ministry with a group drawn from China, Japan, Indonesia, India and the U.K., will inevitably bring a range of information and perspectives about what happens in church life that can stimulate deeper reflection on ministry styles.

Ministry placements are largely conducted by students on their own, but their reflections and feedback are shared with local mentors and staff, bringing a wealth of culturally informed analyses to bear on what is happening. Mission trips allow students to enter more deeply into another culture and to share this experience as a multicultural team. A wide range of contact with staff, fellow-students, and south-east Asian cultures allows for a rich tapestry of experiences and opportunities for staff and peer-mentoring.

Further Reading on Contextual Learning across Cultures

Banks, R. *Re-envisioning Theological Education: Exploring a Missional Alternative to Current Models.* Grand Rapids, MI: Eerdmans, 2000.
Esterline, D. V. and Ogbu U. Kalu (eds.) *Shaping Beloved Community: Multicultural Theological Education.* Louisville, KY: Westminster/John Knox Press, 2006.
Harley, D. *Preparing to Serve.* Pasadena, CA: William Carey Library, 1995.
Taylor, W. E. (ed.) *Internationalizing Missionary Training: a Global Perspective.* Carlisle: Paternoster, 1991.

Educational Elements of Contextual Learning

Culture influences the learning process and lecturers need to be aware of the way this influences various aspects of educational life. All learning communities and academic disciplines have their own "ethos," and part of the process of becoming a student is to learn not just knowledge and skills, but to know what is expected within the "culture" of the discipline. In a multicultural setting, it is important to articulate the kinds of educational values which are encouraged, both so that students know what is expected and to pre-empt misunderstandings; it can also be helpful to try to anticipate or predict how cultural norms will shape the way that students behave and for the community to discuss this periodically during the academic year.

Contextual learning in an Asian setting

Teaching students from different south-east Asian cultures means being conscious of differences in academic culture and social contexts, and consciously taking account of the impact of cultural, economic and technological factors. Students coming from places like Singapore and Myanmar may have a very different appreciation, when they first arrive, of the scope and potential of resources like the Internet. The extent to which students are encouraged to reflect current scholarship (as mediated by their own as well as by their lecturer's views) and the stage at which creativity and originality are deeply encouraged, also seems to vary across cultures.

Our community (and others in Singapore) has found it helpful to outline in a special course on "Study Skills" what exactly is expected from students in their assignments and coursework. Such introductions to the process of study allow for discussion of the role and behaviour of lecturers and students in class; they can explore how learning can derive from the lecturer's teaching, from student interactions and participation, and so on. They can explore learning as collaboration and the place of small group and interactive activities. Such courses can explore the ways in which alternative models of learning and assessment can be effective and how culture affects perceptions of efficacy.

Contextual learning and student participation

Educational factors, combined with cultural values and the level of facility in English, will also have a marked impact on the kind of participation which is possible in the classroom. Those from Asian cultures that stress "saving face" can be hesitant about contributing in settings that are uncertain or where outcomes are poorly or vaguely defined. Personally, I have found that there are ways to facilitate participation, even allowing for a certain cultural caution. In addition to addressing issues of mindset, there are many practical ways to help students to be able to engage more fully. The lecturer can prepare handouts in advance (so students can check unfamiliar vocabulary); they can structure activities in a way that gives an opportunity for periodic checking and summarizing of the flow of material (again to help those whose listening skills are weaker); lecturers can allow groups to work in smaller units of two to four people (where uncertainties can be clarified by peers) before coming back to the class as a whole. For example, when teaching classes on Old Testament exegesis, I would prepare handouts for the following week that would indicate potential linguistic issues, note some key words and concepts, and give space for reflection on theological issues and the section as a whole. Students would have time to work on these on their own with relevant commentaries and books. During the class, there would be time for a briefing as to what was going on for the specific class; there was time for small groups; an intermediate discussion to check all had really grasped what was going on;

further small group work and then, and only then, would we interact as a class.

Such approaches may seem slightly artificial, or even stilted, and certainly need space for students and lecturer to take material in creative directions, but they were considerably more effective than sessions that offered too *few* parameters. One colleague, who was Asian-American ran a very successful course on "group dynamics" with a high degree of class participation, using methods from Asia and beyond which often led to new experiences for students; this lecturer took time to explain the nature of the course and carefully debriefed the students at the end of each participatory activity. Students enjoyed participating in these activities, an enjoyment heightened by their relative unfamiliarity – however, they did not feel that they were being put into *intolerably* ambiguous situations. It is important in a multicultural learning community to design learning activities in such a way that students from different cultures will feel comfortable in the classroom.

Contextual learning and a syllabus for Asia

At DTC, we affirm connecting learning to the Asian settings of our students and we have realized that there are a number of levels at which courses can be connected to local contexts. The syllabus can reflect local, as well as (or instead of), global issues; readings can be chosen which show the importance of local contributions to the discipline; assignments can be designed to connect with the student's own cultural backgrounds; where materials are scarce or non-existent, students can be encouraged to think about how gaps might merit further research at a later stage, or how a project on existing parallels in neighbouring or global contexts could be used as a springboard for future research. To avoid the kind of dislocation mentioned by Sugitharajah and Mbiti, lecturers can seek to design courses in a practical way that allows connections to be made. One theologian has stressed that "… there needs to be a real willingness to simply connect with the local context and local practitioners."[25] In the same way, lecturers can choose to make connections to the local context with examples, with assignments, and with the way in which material is applied to the student's own experience.[26]

---

[25] M. Daniel Carroll, "Perspectives on Teaching the Old Testament from the Two Thirds World," In *Make the Old Testament Live: From Curriculum to Classroom.* (2nd ed.), ed. by Richard S. Hess and Gordon J. Wenham (Grand Rapids, MI: Eerdmans, 1998), 153-155.

[26] This focus on local context did not exclude global concerns, but it *did* involve giving students a choice to pick situations of interest or relevance to them whether relating to their own culture at home or in diaspora communities in S.E. Asia where possible and where literature or case studies existed (or where they themselves felt able to undertake research to bridge the gaps in terms of existing materials.)

Subject areas and courses can be designed in a way that resolutely reflects an emphasis on Asian themes. In addition to diverse connections to the Asian context, the DTC syllabus has had a whole section on Asia which comprised courses on Asian Church History; Asian Religions; Asian Theology and Asian Hermeneutics; Asian Mission Movements and Asian Society. An effort has been made to encourage those courses to be taught by Asian staff (even where international staff shared in teaching other aspects of the syllabus). Church History is taught with a strong emphasis on the development of churches across Asia, picking up on recent research that shows the importance of church movements from before 1500, as well as the expansion of the church from 1500 onwards, including, but not limited to its interactions with the European colonial powers.[27] Courses on religions emphasize the rise, history and influence of the Asian religions such as Chinese Religions, Hinduism, Buddhism and Islam. These religions often have a different ethos and character depending on their specific cultural setting and many pose formidable challenges in terms of Christian apologetics.

There are also courses on Asian theology and local theology which look at ways in which the social and religious forces in Asian society, as well as the discipline of theological studies (and the history of the church in Asia), have shaped the theological agenda. Recent surveys on Asian theology have reminded us both of the necessity and limitations of work to date in terms of theology for Asia and theology derived from Asia. Interaction with scholars and their writings in these fields needs to be an integral part of a theological syllabus in Asia.[28] Moonjang Lee, a Korean theologian who has worked in Singapore and taught in the area of Asian theology, has extended his interests to the field of biblical hermeneutics in Asia. Lee is concerned to show that there is a new era in biblical studies and interpretation – he calls it a time for a "post-critical reading of the bible" – a time for new approaches to these fields that have a fresh relevance for Asia. His own approach to teaching at DTC centred around helping Asian students to connect the western tradition of biblical interpretation to what could be called alternative interpretive styles or traditions in Asia.[29]

---

[27] There are a number of materials available – see, for example, Samuel H. Moffett, *A History of Christianity in Asia (Vol.1): Beginnings to 1550* (Maryknoll, N.Y.:Orbis, 2001).

[28] Recent critiques and evaluations of Asian theology include those by Chua, How Chuang, "Asian Theology," in *Dictionary of Mission Theology.* edited by John Corrie (Leicester: IVP, 2007) and Moonjang Lee, "Asian Theology," in *Global Dictionary of Theology: a Resource for the Worldwide Church*, ed. by W. Dyrness and Veli-Matti Karkkainen (Downers Grove, IL: Inter Varsity Press, 2008).

[29] A good introduction to Lee's concerns about hermeneutics are found in Moonjang Lee, "A Post-Critical Reading of the Bible," *Asia Journal of Theology* 14 (2) (2000): 272-285 and Moonjang Lee, "Identifying an Asian Theology," *Asia Journal of Theology* 13 (2) (1999): 256-275.

For contexts in Asia, contextualization is far from being an exotic task and rather involves steady reflection on forms of worship, patterns of evangelism and so on. Courses on "Gospel and Culture" allow for an exploration of the interplay between text and context, not just as a "missional" experience but as a mainstream part of the church's task in Asia as it seeks to make relevant the Christian faith – given that many theological resources are derived from non-Asian contexts. For example, when it comes to the theology of family life, much of the English language literature on Christian family, marital life, and patterns of friendship and courtship, is rooted in the patterns of western cultures.

The Asian context and Asian values

There is sometimes a perception that the widespread advent of technology, where people can watch western films, and internet sites, means that the whole world – at least the "educated world" – is moving to a shared postmodern culture. The realities, however, are more complex and part of the fabric of thriving Asian societies is the new-found confidence of neo-Confucian models based on "Asian values." The Confucian perspective on different levels of relationship has a significant and deep grip on many Asian cultures and Christians need to engage with this from an Asian standpoint rather than depending on ideas coming from the west.[30]

The rise of missionary movements from majority world countries, and particularly Asia, has been another fertile source of material for mission studies. Analysis of the significant mission movement from Mizoram in North-East India, has encouraged students from neighbouring countries and places like Cambodia to look at parallels with the emerging mission movements in their own context, concerning issues like training and finance. Students have been able to bring research skills developed in other fields to bear on a range of topics: the rise of mission movements like those in contemporary Japan and in Myanmar in the nineteenth century; preaching in Chinese contexts; the contextualization of church and worship in parts of Asia where little written material exists on themes like contextualization.

BOOK IDEA

Harkness, Allan (ed.) *Tending the Seedbeds: Educational Perspectives on Theological Education in Asia.* Quezon City, Philippines: Asia Theological Association, 2010.

---

[30] For an introduction to this discussion, see Greig Sheridan, *Asian Values, Western Dreams: Understanding the New Asia* (St. Leonards, N.S.W.: Allen & Unwin, 1999).

This volume puts a strong emphasis on the need for contextual learning communities to connect faculty as well as students to the local Asian settings and the local church contexts in Asia. At an educational level, this includes reflection on Asian views of knowledge and teaching methods, including the challenges of the internet age; at a pastoral level, this extends to an interest in Asian forms of Christianity and the relational character of Asian cultures. The formation of leaders for Asian contexts is a theme that also receives considerable attention.

Asian Cultures Embraced
in a Contextual Worshipping Community

Worship is another area of Christian life where it can be difficult to create a genuine sense of cross-cultural participation that truly represents a number of different traditions. Michael Hawn has written a very insightful article on this theme, in the context of the North American church, and how it can integrate or embrace those from cultures outside the Euro-North American sphere. He describes the issue in terms of the search for appropriate "liturgical plurality" rather than enforcing "cultural uniformity in liturgy."[31] Although Hawn is looking at one particular setting, the issues will be similar to those faced by theological institutions in cosmopolitan cities in many continents all over the world.

Asian cultures and worship – towards 'liturgical plurality'

Promoting multicultural worship needs to address the following issues: the kinds of *liturgical styles* that are adopted; how to deal with *language barriers*; the choice of styles or traditions of *music* that are adopted; and how culture affects a range of factors from the use of physical space to inter-personal interactions. At DTC, we have come to realize that these issues are not easy to deal with, and needed to be treated wholistically. As a result, we made the decision to introduce two weeks in every quarter where a particular culture was to be emphasized. Worship times during this week would reflect the emphases of this culture, and we made it possible for our extended Wednesday morning service to be significantly shaped by liturgical and other elements from the selected culture. In practice, this allowed for some additional features such as meal-times and dress during those weeks highlighting the culture in question. In our Singaporean

---

[31] The author read Hawn's account several years after he had started working at DTC, but the quest for "liturgical plurality" seems to express very well the search

setting, Indian sub-continent dress (like *salwar kameez, dhotis,* or *saris*) and Indonesian or Malaysian dress could easily be adopted by quite a number of students and staff. Community meal-times embraced cuisine from different Asian cultures, and the weeks show-casing Korean, Thai and Malaysian (Indonesian) food and drinks were particularly popular!

The physical layout of a room, the degree of formality of the seating (or lack of seats), the mixing or separation of the sexes, the formalities marking the space for those leading worship – these are all issues that need to be considered in multicultural worship. Some cultures tend to favour service time marked by formal liturgical elements; others are relatively free. On weeks when worship was led by those from the Indian sub-continent, or by Korean members of the community, it tended to have more formal elements, with the person leading worship standing at a lectern and using liturgical elements in a more tightly structured service. By contrast, services led by those from South East Asian cultures, could be more interactive. In some cases, we explored how cultures that sit on the floor might conduct worship in a more informal setting. In contexts like DTC, where English is the *lingua franca,* when another Asian language is required for an Asian service, there are a number of devices which could be used to include the language. Biblical passages could be read in both the Asian language and English; short and simple liturgical elements could be taught to the congregation before the service or used with translation (written or on a screen); one verse of a song (or the chorus) could be in a local language with the other verses translated into English. These simple adjustments help to reflect the cultural diversity that exists in Asia and bring it into the midst of the learning community in its times of worship.

Further Reading on "Liturgical Plurality"

Conde-Frazier, E., S. Steve Kang and G. A. Parrett. *A Many Colored Kingdom: Multicultural Dynamics for Spiritual Formation.* Grand Rapids, MI: Baker Academic, 2004.

Farhadian, C. (ed.) *Christian Worship Worldwide: Expanding Horizons, Deepening Practices.* Grand Rapids, MI: Eerdmans, 2007.

Farlee, R.B., P. Westermeyer and M. P. Bangert. *Leading the Church's Song: A Practical Introduction to Leading Congregational Song.* Kitchener, ON: Augsburg Fortress, 2011.

Hawn, C. Michael. *Gather into One: Singing and Praying Globally.* Grand Rapids, MI: Eerdmans, 2003.

Marti G. *Worship across the Racial Divide: Religious Music and the Multiracial Congregation.* Oxford: OUP, 2012.

Integrating local music for worship in Asian contexts

Music is another important area to consider. In some cultures, like Korea and Japan, the local churches have consciously and decisively chosen to adopt the European tradition (with more limited use of distinctive local music); in other cultures, like Pakistan and Thailand, local traditions are very strong. We decided to adopt a pragmatic, but culturally nuanced approach. We identified a small number of songs from each culture in our community; we collected the relevant music and words; we translated texts into English or kept local words if they were simple enough. Staff and students were encouraged to use those hymns and songs to supplement more traditional music in regular use, especially, but not exclusively during the special weeks emphasizing different cultures. (We avoided using the piano where it was inappropriate for certain musical styles, encouraging guitar, melody instruments or *a cappella* singing instead – sometimes percussion instruments were used, with small drums helping to maintain the rhythmic pulse and vitality that are an intrinsic part of certain kinds of Asian music.)[32]

Allowing for all the complexities and limitations of this approach, it achieved a number of goals: students realized that not only were all cultures affirmed and welcomed in the DTC community, but that the contribution of the church from each of these cultures had a role to play in our worship and in contributing towards "liturgical plurality." It was clear, however, that for certain students, being able to sing songs or adopt liturgical forms which were familiar to them, really empowered them and helped them to feel "at home" in worship and in the community.

Conclusion

We have discussed various aspects of a multicultural learning community in the context of the Discipleship Training Centre in Singapore. We have explored ways in which the community has tried to take account of the various cultural backgrounds of the students and to value their contributions to the community. In terms of Asian cultures, we have seen that relationships are important and that lecturers can learn to be mentors in effective ways that preserve Asian cultural sensitivities and we have

---

[32] The above approach is possible without training in ethno-musicology, but it requires planning and some familiarity with the European musical tradition and an interest in Asian musical systems and their general characteristics. A practical and informed guide is found in R.B. Farlee, P. Westermeyer and M. P. Bangert, *Leading the Church's Song: A Practical Introduction to Leading Congregational Song.* (Kitchener, ON: Augsburg Fortress, 2011) – see especially the section on Asia. For a deeper exploration of musical and cultural issues in Asia, see I-to Loh, "Music, Asian Christian," in *A Dictionary of Asian Christianity,* ed. by Scott W. Sunquist (Grand Rapids, MI: Eerdmans, 2001), 569-574. A recent introduction to Dr. Loh and his work can be found in Michael Nai Poon, "Loh I-to as Bridge-Builder: Communication and communion in the Asia Pacific." Teologia 50 (1) 2012:54-65, http://www.revistateologia.ro/downloads/Teologia/teologia_1_2012.pdf (accessed 8th February 2016).

indicated various ways in which the theological syllabus can be connected to Asia. We have considered ways in which the worship and corporate life of the community can be enriched by the cultural and Christian heritage of Asian communities. We hope that these ideas will be of relevance to educators in Asia and to those who encounter Asian students in other contexts, recognizing that they simply reflect one community's experiences.

At DTC, we seek to embrace and empower a small, but dedicated band of pilgrims, who have made their own contributions over forty years to the church in Asia and beyond. Their identity as followers of Jesus Christ has been shaped by their time in a learning community in Singapore, which has prepared them for service and ministry, and helped them to be deeply conscious of the bonds that connect disciples from different cultures to others in the community of the kingdom.

Questions for Reflection/Discussion

1. In a culture known to you, how does the use of language and/ or vocabulary reflect distinctive cultural perspectives on a) relationships between students and teachers and b) relationships between different groups, ages or genders of students? What impact might this have on "learning relationships" in the classroom and beyond?
2. How easily do concepts of "mentoring" cross cultural boundaries? Can you think of situations where typical patterns of staff-student mentoring may need to be adjusted to help certain members of the student body?
3. Think of courses where you have been a student or a teacher: in what ways could the themes of the course have been connected to local authors or local problems in your culture? Where little local writing or research exists, what topics might prove especially fruitful for further research?
4. In the context of a training programme or an educational community – how could the different groups represented be given opportunities to shape worship according to their cultures? In what ways might particular elements – such as liturgical forms, music, physical settings, or styles of sharing God's word – raise difficulties in terms of being accessible to those from different cultural groups?

BIBLIOGRAPHY

"Constructing a worldview." https://orality.imb.org/resources/?id=148 (accessed 8th February 2016)

"Which Evangelism Approach should I use?" *Ministry Advantage* (Fuller Theological Seminary) 7 (3) Summer 1997: 6.

Acoba, E. (et al). *Doing Theology in the Philippines.* Manila: OMF Literature, 2005.

Adeney, Bernard. *Strange Virtues: Ethics in a Multicultural World.* Downers Grove, IL: Inter Varsity Press, 1995.

Anderson, Gerald H. *Asian Voices in Christian Theology.* Maryknoll, NY: Orbis, 1976.

Banks, Robert. *Re-envisioning Theological Education: Exploring a Missional Alternative to Current Models.* Grand Rapids, MI: Eerdmans, 2000.

Beasley-Murray, I. "Revelation, Book of." In *Dictionary of the Later New Testament and Its Developments.* Edited by Ralph Martin, and Peter H. Davids. Downers Grove, IL: Inter Varsity Press, 1997, 1028.

Beattie, Stroma. "Enhancing Member Care in the Singapore Context: Towards Good Practice and the Resolution of Problematic Issues." *Missions Matrix: Navigating 21st Century Missiological Issues.* Edited by Florence Tan, 103-133. Singapore: Singapore Bible College, 2009.

Beattie, Warren R. "Learning Lessons from an Asian Church Leader." In *Global Mission: Reflections and Case studies in Contextualization for the Whole Church.* Edited by Rose Dowsett, 85-96. Pasadena, CA: William Carey Library 2011.

Bevans, Stephens. *Models of Contextual Theology.* (Rev. and expanded edition). Maryknoll, N.Y.: Orbis, 2002.

Bosch, David. *Transforming Mission,* Maryknoll: Orbis, 1991.

Branson, Mark L. and Juan F. Martinez. *Church, Cultures and Leadership: a Practical Theology of Congregations and Ethnicities.* Downers Grove, IL: IVP Academic, 2011.

Brawley, Robert L. "Teaching the Bible in a Global Context." In *Shaping Beloved Community: Multicultural Theological Education.* Edited by David V. Esterline and Ogbu U. Kalu, 113 – 127. Louisville, KY: Westminster/John Knox Press, 2006.

Burke, David. "Time to Leave the Wilderness? The Teaching of Pastoral Theology in South East Asia." In *Tending the Seedbeds: Educational Perspectives on Theological Education in Asia.* Edited by Allan Harkness, 263-284. Quezon City, Philippines: Asia Theological Association, 2010.

Burnett, David. *Clash of Worlds.* Crowborough: MARC, 1990.

Caldwell, Larry W. "How Asian is Asian Theological Education?" In *Tending the Seedbeds: Educational Perspectives on Theological Education in Asia.* Edited by Allan Harkness, 23-46. Quezon City, Philippines: Asia Theological Association, 2010.

Carroll, M. Daniel. "Perspectives on Teaching the Old Testament from the Two Thirds World," In *Make the Old Testament Live: From Curriculum to Classroom.* (2nd ed.) Edited by Richard S. Hess and Gordon J. Wenham, 144 – 160. Grand Rapids, MI: Eerdmans, 1998.

Carson, Don. *The Gagging of God.* Grand Rapids, MI: Zondervan, 1996.

Carter, C. A. *Rethinking Christ and Culture: A Post-Christendom Perspective.* Grand Rapids: Brazos Press, 2006.

Chan, Simon. "Evangelical Theology in Asian Contexts." In *The Cambridge Companion to Evangelical Theology.* (Cambridge Companions to Religion). Edited by Timothy Larsen and Daniel J. Treier, 225 – 240. Cambridge: CUP, 2007.

Chang, P. "Steak, Potatoes, Peas and Chopsuey: Linear and Non-Linear Thinking in Theological Education." *Evangelical Review of Theology* 5(2) 1981:279-286.

Chew, Jim. *When You Cross Cultures.* (2nd ed.) Singapore: Nav Media, 2009.

Chua, How Chuang. "Asian Theology". In *Dictionary of Mission Theology.* Edited by John Corrie. Leicester: IVP, 2007.

Coe, Shoki. "Contextualising Theology." in *Third World Theologies.* (Trends in Mission vol. 3). Edited by G.H. Anderson, and T. E. Stransky, 19-24. Grand Rapids, MI: Eerdmans, 1973.

Cole, Graham. "Do Christians have a worldview?" http://tgc-documents.s3.amazonaws.com/cci/Cole.pdf (accessed 8th February 2016).

Coleman, Robert. "Evangelism" In *Evangelical Dictionary of World Missions.* Edited by Scott A. Moreau, Grand Rapids, MI: Baker Books, 2000.

Cook, Matthew, Rob Haskell, Ruth Julian & Natee Tanchanpongs. *Local Theology for the Global Church: Principles for an Evangelical Approach to Contextualization.* Pasadena, CA: William Carey Library 2010.

Conde-Frazier, Elizabeth, S. Steve Kang and Gary A. Parrett. *A Many Colored Kingdom: Multicultural Dynamics for Spiritual Formation.* Grand Rapids, MI: Baker Academic, 2004.

Corrie, John (ed.) *Dictionary of Mission Theology.* Leicester: IVP, 2007.

Courson, Jim. "Deepening the Bonds of Christian Community: applying Rite of Passage Structure to the Discipling Process in Taiwan." *Missiology: An International Review.* 26 (3) 1998: 301-313.

Day, Jackson. *Bible Storytelling Tools. A Guide for Storying the Bible.* Opelika, AL: Jack Day, 2007.

de Mesa, J. "Doing Theology as Inculturation in the Asian Context." In *New Directions in Mission and Evangelisation. Vol 3. Faith and Culture.* J.A. Scherer, and S. B. Bevans (eds.), 117-133. NY: Orbis, 1999.

Dillon, Christine. *Telling the Gospel Through Story: Evangelism That Keeps Hearers Wanting More,* Leicester: IVP, 2012.

Douglas, Mary. *Natural Symbols: Explorations in Cosmology.* London: Barrie and Rockcliff, 1970.

Dowsett, Rose (ed). *Global Mission: Reflections and Case studies.* Pasadena, CA: William Carey Library 2011.

Dyrness, William. *Themes in Old Testament Theology.* Cape Town: Oxford University Press, 1979.

Dyrness, William and Veli-Matti Karkkainen (eds.) *Global Dictionary of Theology: a Resource for the Worldwide Church.* Downers Grove, IL: Inter Varsity Press, 2008.

Eims, Leroy. *The Lost Art of Disciple Making.* Grand Rapids, MI: Zondervan, 1978.

Elmer, Duane. *Cross-cultural Conflict: Building Relationships for Effective Ministry.* Downers Grove, IL: IVP Academic, 1993.

Esterline, David V. and Ogbu U. Kalu (eds.) *Shaping Beloved Community: Multicultural Theological Education.* Louisville, KY: Westminster/John Knox Press, 2006.

Esterline, David V. "Multicultural theological education and leadership for a church without walls." In *Shaping Beloved Community: Multicultural Theological Education.* Edited by David V. Esterline and Ogbu U. Kalu, 15 – 27. Louisville, KY: Westminster/John Knox Press, 2006.

Falls, Thomas (ed.) *Saint Justin Martyr.* New York: Christian Heritage, 1949.

Farhadian, Charles. (ed.) *Christian Worship Worldwide: Expanding Horizons, Deepening Practices.* Grand Rapids: Eerdmans, 2007.

Farlee, R.B., P. Westermeyer and M. P. Bangert. *Leading the Church's Song: A Practical Introduction to Leading Congregational Song.* Kitchener, ON: Augsburg Fortress, 2011.

Fernando, Ajith. "The Church: the Mirror of the Trinity." In *Global Missiology for the 21ˢᵗ Century.* Edited by William Taylor, 239-256. Grand Rapids, MI: World Evangelical Fellowship, 2000.

Flemming, Dean. *Contextualization in the New Testament: Patterns for Theology and Mission.* Downers Grove, IL: Intervarsity Press, 2005.

Fuller, Harold W. *Church-Mission Dynamics.* Pasadena, CA: William Carey Library, 1980.

Futrell, Mynga. "Worldview Diversity" Teaching about Religion: in Support of Civic Pluralism. http://www.teachingaboutreligion.org/worldviewdiversity.html (accessed 8th February 2016).

Geertz, Clifford. *Interpretation of Cultures: Selected Essays.* New York: Basic Books, 1973.

Geffre, C. "Christianity and Culture." *International Review of Mission* 84(332/333) 1995:17-31.

Gehring, Roger W. *House Church and Mission.* Grand Rapids: Eerdmans, 2004.

Gilliland, Dean. "Contextual Theology as Incarnation Mission" in *The Word Among Us: Contextualizing Theology for Mission Today.* Edited by Dean Gilliland, 5-19. Waco: Word, 1989.

Gittins, Anthony. J. "Anthropology." In *Dictionary of Mission: Theology, History, Perspectives* edited by K. Müller, T. Sundermeier, S. B. Bevans and R. H. Bliese, 23-8. Maryknoll N.Y.: Orbis Books, 1997.

Gittins, Anthony. *Ministry at the Margins: Strategy and Spirituality for Mission.* Maryknoll, N.Y.: Orbis Books, 2002.

Gnanakan, Ken (ed.) *Biblical Theology in Asia.* Bangalore: Theological Book Trust, 1995.

Gorringe, Timothy. J. *Furthering Humanity: a Theology of Culture.* Aldershot: Ashgate, 2004.

Green, Michael. *Evangelism in the Early Church.* (Revised Edition). Grand Rapids: Eerdmans, 2003.

Green, Michael. *Acts for Today.* London: Hodder and Stoughton, 1993.

Harkness, Allan (ed.) *Tending the Seedbeds: Educational Perspectives on Theological Education in Asia.* Quezon City, Philippines: Asia Theological Association, 2010.

Harley, David. *Preparing to Serve: Training for Cross-Cultural Mission.* Pasadena, CA: William Carey Library, 1995.

Harley, David. "Critical Issues in Contextual Discipleship." *Mission Round Table: the Occasional Bulletin of OMF Mission Research* 1(2) 2005: 20-22.

Hawn, C. Michael. "Praying Globally – Pitfalls and Possibilities of Cross-cultural Liturgical Appropriation." In *Christian Worship Worldwide: Expanding*

Horizons, Deepening Practices. Edited by C. Farhadian, 205–230. Grand Rapids: W.B. Eerdmans, 2007.

Hawn, C. Michael. *Gather into One: Singing and Praying Globally.* Grand Rapids, MI: Eerdmans, 2003.

Hess, Richard S. and Gordon J. Wenham (eds.) *Make the Old Testament Live: From Curriculum to Classroom.* (2nd ed.) Grand Rapids, MI: Eerdmans, 1998.

Hesselgrave, David J. and Edward Rommen. *Contextualization: Meanings, Methods and Models.* Pasadena, CA: William Carey Library, 2000.

Hesselgrave, David J. *Communicating Christ Cross-Culturally: an Introduction to Missionary Communication.* (2nd ed.) Grand Rapids, MI: Zondervan, 1991.

Hesselgrave. David J. *Planting Churches Cross-Culturally: North America and Beyond.* (2nd ed.) Grand Rapids: Baker Academic, 2000.

Hiebert, Paul. "Critical Contextualization." *International Bulletin of Missionary Research* 11(3) 1987:104-12.

Hiebert, Paul & Frances Hiebert. *Case Studies in Mission.* Grand Rapids, MI: Baker, 1987.

Hiebert, Paul. *Anthropological Insights for Missionaries.* Grand Rapids, MI: Baker, 1985.

Hiebert, Paul. *Transforming Worldviews: an Anthropological Understanding of how People Change.* Grand Rapids, MI: Baker Academic, 2008.

Hiebert, Theodore, Jennifer Blandford, Andrew Davis, Hardy Kim. "The Tower of Babel and Cultural Diversity: A Case Study on Engaging Diversity in the Classroom." In *Shaping Beloved Community: Multicultural Theological Education.* Edited by David V. Esterline and Ogbu U. Kalu, 128 – 141. Louisville, KY: Westminster/John Knox Press, 2006.

Hkaw, Sau. "3/300 Mission of Kachin Baptist Convention." Unpublished Masters Thesis. Burma Institute of Theology, Yangon, Myanmar, 1990.

Hoefer, H. "Rooted or Uprooted: The Necessity of Contextualization in Missions." *International Journal of Frontier Missions* 24(3) 2007: 131-8.

Howard, Douglas. "Measuring Contexualization in Church and Missions." *International Journal of Frontier Missions.* Vol 12 (3) July-Sep. 1995: 135-138.

Hwa, Yung. *Beyond AD 2000. A Call to Evangelical Faithfulness.* Kuala Lumpur: Kairos Research Centre, 1999.

Hwa Yung. *Bribery and Corruption: Biblical Reflections and Case Studies for the Marketplace in Asia.* (Truth for life Series edited by Soo-Inn Tan). Singapore: Graceworks, 2010.

Hwa, Yung. *Mangoes or Bananas.* Regnum: Oxford, 1997.

Irizarry, Jose R. "Toward an intercultural approach to theological education for ministry." In *Shaping Beloved Community: Multicultural Theological Education.* Edited by David V. Esterline and Ogbu U. Kalu, 27-42. Louisville, KY: Westminster/John Knox Press, 2006.

Jenkins, Philip. *The New Faces of Christianity: Believing the Bible in the Global South.* Oxford: New York: Oxford University Press, 2006.

Jenkins, Philip. *The Next Christendom: The Coming of Global Christianity.* (Rev. and expanded edition.) Oxford: Oxford University Press, 2007.

Kalu, Ogbu U. "Multicultural theological education in a non-western context: Africa, 1975 – 2000. In *Shaping Beloved Community: Multicultural Theological Education.* Edited by David V. Esterline and Ogbu U. Kalu, 225 – 242. Louisville, KY: Westminster/John Knox Press, 2006.

Koyama, Kosuke. *Three Mile an Hour God: Biblical Reflections*. Orbis: Maryknoll, NY: 1980.

Koyama, Kosuke. *Waterbuffalo Theology*. Maryknoll, NY: Orbis. 1974.

Kraft, Charles. *Anthropology for Christian Witness*. Maryknoll, NY: Orbis, 1996.

Kraft, Charles. *Christianity in Culture: a Study in Dynamic Biblical Theologizing in Cross Cultural Perspective*. (Revised 25th anniversary ed.) Maryknoll, N.Y.: Orbis Books, 2004.

Kraft, Charles and D. S. Gilliland. 2005. *Appropriate Christianity*. Pasadena, Calif.: William Carey Library.

Kroeber, A. L. and C. Kluckhohn. "Culture: A Critical Review of Concepts and Definition." *Papers of the Peabody Museum of American Archaeology and Ethnology* 47 (1). Cambridge, MA: Harvard University, 1952.

Latourette, Kenneth. *History of Christianity*. (Vol. 2). N.Y.: Harper & Row, 1953.

Lausanne Committee on World Evangelization. "The Lausanne Covenant." https://www.lausanne.org/content/covenant/lausanne-covenant (accessed 8th February 2016).

Lausanne Committee on World Evangelization. Lausanne Occasional Paper 2: "The Willowbank Report – Consultation on Gospel and Culture, 1978".) https://www.lausanne.org/content/lop/lop-2 (accessed 8th February 2016).

Lederleitner, Mary T. *Cross-Cultural Partnerships – Navigating the Complexities of Money and Mission*. Downers Grove, IL: Inter Varsity Press, 2010.

Lee, Kwang Soon and Young Won Lee. *Introduction to Missiology (Seon-gyo-hak gae-ron)*, Seoul: Presbyterian Publishing, 1993. (In Korean).

Lee, Moonjang. "A Post-Critical Reading of the Bible." *Asia Journal of Theology* 14 (2) (2000): 272-285.

Lee, Moonjang. "Identifying an Asian Theology." *Asia Journal of Theology* 13 (2) (1999):256-275.

Lee, Moonjang. "Asian Theology" In *Global Dictionary of Theology: a Resource for the Worldwide Church*. Edited by W. Dyrness and Veli-Matti Karkkainen. Downers Grove, IL: Inter Varsity Press, 2008.

Legrand, Lucien. *The Bible on Culture*. (Faith and Cultures Series.) Maryknoll, N.Y.: Orbis Books, 2000.

Lingenfelter, Sherwood and M.K. Mayers. *Ministering Cross-Culturally: an Incarnational Model for Personal Relationships*. Grand Rapids, MI: Baker, 2003.

Lingenfelter, Judith E. *Teaching Cross-Culturally: an Incarnational Model for Learning and Teaching*. Grand Rapids, MI: Baker, 2005.

Loh I-to. "Music, Asian Christian." In *A Dictionary of Asian Christianity*. Edited by Scott W. Sunquist, 569-574. Grand Rapids, MI: Eerdmans, 2001.

Luzbetak, Louis J. "Anthropology and Mission." In *Dictionary of Mission: Theology, History, Perspectives*. Edited by K. Müller, T. Sundermeier, S. B. Bevans and R. H. Bliese, 28-30. Maryknoll: Orbis Books, 2007.

Maggay, Melba. *The Gospel in Filipino Context*. Manila: OMF Literature, 1987.

Maggay, M. *Jew to the Jew and Greek to the Greek: Reflections on Culture and Globalization*. Manila: ISACC, 2001.

Martin, Ralph and Peter H. Davids (ed.) *Dictionary of the Later New Testament and Its Developments*. Downers Grove, IL: Inter Varsity Press, 1997.

Matthews, C. T. "Culture." In *The Blackwell Companion to Modern Theology*. Edited by G. Jones, 47-64. Malden, MA ; Oxford, UK: Blackwell, 2004.

Mbiti, John. "Theological Impotence and the Universality of the Church." In *Mission Trends No 3: Third World Theologies.* Edited by G.H. Anderson, and T. E. Stransky, 6-18. New York: Paulist Press & Grand Rapids, MI: Eerdmans, 1976.

McLuhan, Marshall and Quentin Fiore. *The Medium is the Massage: an Inventory of Effects* London: Penguin Modern Classics, 2008. [1st ed. 1967].

Mejudhon, Nanthachai. "Meekness: A New Approach to Christian Witness to the Thai People" Unpublished Doctor of Missiology Thesis, Asbury Theological Seminary, Wilmore, Kentucky, U.S.A.,1997.

Michell, Brian J. "Leadership development and transition in missionary partnership and closure: observations from the OMF/Borneo Evangelical Mission (BEM) Experience in East Malaysia." *Mission Round Table: the Occasional Bulletin of OMF Mission Research* 3(1) 2007: 2-8.

Michell, Brian J. "The Role of Missionary Partnership and Closure in Indigenous Church Development: A Malaysian Case Study." Unpublished Doctor of Missiology Thesis, Asian Graduate School of Theology, Manila, the Philippines, 2004.

Miranda-Feliciano, Evelyn. *Filipino Values and our Christian Faith.* Manila: OMF Literature, 1990.

Moffett, Samuel H. *A History of Christianity in Asia (Vol.1). Beginnings to 1550.* Maryknoll, N.Y.:Orbis, 2001.

Moffett, Samuel H. *A History of Christianity in Asia (Vol.2). 1500 to 1900.* Maryknoll, N.Y.:Orbis, 2005.

Naugle, David K. *Worldview: the History of a Concept.* Grand Rapids, MI: Eerdmans, 2002.

Nicholls, Bruce J. "Contextualization in Chinese Culture." *Evangelical Review of Theology.* 19 (4) 1995:368-380.

Nicholls, Bruce. J. *Contextualization: a Theology of Gospel and Culture.* Downers Grove, IL: Intervarsity Press, 1979.

Niebuhr, H. Reinhold. *Christ and Culture.* New York: Harper & Row, 1951.

Nunnenmacher, E. "Culture." In *Dictionary of Mission: Theology, History, Perspectives.* Edited by K. Müller, T. Sundermeier, S. B. Bevans and R. H. Bliese, 94-8. Maryknoll, N.Y.: Orbis Books, 1997.

Ott, Craig and G. Wilson. *Global Church Planting: Biblical Principles and Best Practices for Multiplication.* Grand Rapids, MI: Baker, 2011.

Payne, Ian. "Reproducing Leaders Through Mentoring." In *Tending the Seedbeds: Educational Perspectives on Theological Education in Asia.* Edited by Allan Harkness, 167-192. Quezon City, Philippines: Asia Theological Association, 2010.

Payne, J.D. *Discovering Church Planting: An Introduction to the Whats, Whys, and Hows of Global Church Planting.* Downers Grove, IL: IVP, 2009.

Poon, Michael Nai. "Loh I-to as Bridge-Builder: Communication and communion in the Asia Pacific." Teologia 50 (1) 2012:54-65. http://www.revistateologia.ro/downloads/Teologia/teologia_1_2012.pdf (Accessed 8th February 2016).

Peskett, Howard and Vinoth Ramachandra The Message of Mission (The Bible speaks today) Leicester: IVP, 2003.

Plueddemann, James E. *Leading Across Cultures: Effective Ministry and Mission in the Global Church.* Downers Grove, IL: IVP Academic, 2009.

Ramachandra, Vinoth. *Church and Mission in the New Asia.* Singapore: CSCA, 2009.

Ro, Bong Rin, "Contextualization: Asian Theology" in *Biblical Theology in Asia*. Edited by Ken Gnanakan, 3-17. Bangalore: Theological Book Trust, 1995.

Salter, Darius. *American Evangelism*. Grand Rapids, MI: Baker Books, 1996.

Sanneh, Lamin O. *Translating the Message: The Missionary Impact on Culture*. (American Society of Missiology series, No. 13.) Maryknoll, N.Y.: Orbis Books, 1989.

Sanneh, Lamin O. *Whose Religion is Christianity? The Gospel beyond the West*. Grand Rapids, MI: Eerdmans, 2003.

Scherer, James A. and Stephen B. Bevans. *New Directions in Mission & Evangelization (Vol. 3): Faith and Culture*. Maryknoll, N.Y.: Orbis, 1999.

Schreiter, Robert. "Anthropology and Faith." *Missiology: An International Review* 19(3) 1991: 283-94.

Schreiter, Robert. *Constructing Local Theologies*. Maryknoll, NY: Orbis, 1986.

Sedmak, Clemens. *Doing Local Theology*. (Faith and Cultures series). Maryknoll, N.Y.:Orbis Books 2003.

Segal, Allan. *Paul the Convert: The Apostolate and Apostasy of Saul the Pharisee*. New Haven: Yale University Press, 1990.

Senapatiratne, D., S. Allen and R. Bowers. "Folk Buddhism in Southeast Asia." Unpublished pamphlet. Pnomh Phen: Training of Timothy, 2003.

Shaw, Perry W. H. "'New treasures with the Old': Addressing Culture and Gender Imperialism in Higher Level Theological Education." In *Tending the Seedbeds: Educational Perspectives on Theological Education in Asia*. Edited by Allan Harkness, 47-74. Quezon City, Philippines: Asia Theological Association, 2010.

Sheridan, Greg. *Asian Values,Western Dreams: Understanding the New Asia*. St. Leonards, N.S.W.: Allen & Unwin, 1999.

SIB (the Evangelical Church of Borneo). The Minutes of the combined SIB Sabah & Sarawak Komiti Adat-Istiadat (the Evangelical Church of Borneo). Unpublished Minutes, held by the SIB Church, Sabah, East Malaysia. (in Bahasa Malaysia).

Sire, James. *The Universe Next Door*. Downers Grove, IL: Inter Varsity Press , 1988.

Solomon, Robert. *The Conscience: Rediscovering the Inner Compass*. Singapore: Armour, 2010.

Song, Minho. "Contextualization and Discipleship: closing the Gap between Theory and Practice." *Mission Round Table: the Occasional Bulletin of OMF Mission Research* 1 (2) 2005:10-19.

Steffen, Tom A. "How User-Friendly is your Teaching?" *Evangelical Missions Quarterly* 32 (2) 1996: 178-185.

Steffen, Tom A. "Don't Show the Jesus Film." *Evangelical Missions Quarterly* 29(3) 1993:272-275.

Steffen, Tom A. *Passing the Baton: Church Planting That Empowers*. (Rev.Ed.) La Habra, CA: Centre for Organization and Ministry Development, 1997.

Storti, Craig. *The Art of Crossing Cultures*. 2nd ed. Nicholas Brealey Publishing London, 2008.

Stott, John. *The Living Church*. Leicester: IVP, 2007.

Stott, John. (ed.) *Making Christ Known: Historic Mission Documents from the Lausanne Movement 1974-1989*. Cumbria: Paternoster Press, 1996.

Sugirtharajah, R.S. (ed.) *Frontiers in Asian Christian Theology: Emerging Trends*. N.Y.: Orbis, 1994.

Sugirtharajah, R.S. *Postcolonial Reconfigurations: an Alternative Way of Reading the Bible and Doing Theology*. London: SCM, 2003.

Sung, Yao-Hwa E. "Culture and Hermeneutics." In *Dictionary for Theological Interpretation of the Bible*. Edited by K. J. Vanhoozer, C. G. Bartholomew, D. J. Treier and N. T. Wright, 150-5. Grand Rapids, MI: Baker Academic, 2005.

Sunquist, Scott W. (ed.) *A Dictionary of Asian Christianity*. Grand Rapids, MI: Eerdmans, 2001.

Szto, Melville. *Where Your Treasure Is*. Singapore: Genesis Books, Armour Publishing, 2003.

Taber, Charles R. *The World is too Much with Us: "Culture" in Modern Protestant Missions*. Macon: Mercer, 1991.

Tai, J. "Preaching in the Church in China." *Chinese Theological Review* 11 (1) 1996: 21-30.

Tanner, Kathryn. *Theories of Culture: A New Agenda for Theology*. Guides to Theological Inquiry. Minneapolis: Fortress Press, 1997.

Taylor, Steve. "Patron-Client Relationships: A Challenge for the Thai Church." *Mission Round Table: the Occasional Bulletin of OMF Mission Research* 3(1) 2007: 16 – 21.

Taylor, William E. (ed.) *Internationalizing Missionary Training: a Global Perspective*. Carlisle: Paternoster, 1991.

Taylor, William E. (ed.) *Global Missiology for the 21st Century*. Grand Rapids, MI: World Evangelical Fellowship, 2000.

Towns, Elmers and D. Porter. *The Ten Greatest Revivals Ever*. Ann Arbor, MI: Servant Publications, 2000.

Transparency International. *Global Corruption Report 2004: Special Focus – Political Corruption*. London: Pluto Press, 2004.

Tuwere, I. "What is contextual theology: a view from Oceania?" *Pacific Journal of Theology* Series 2 (27) 2002: 7-19.

Van Engen, Charles. *God's Missionary People: Rethinking the Purpose of the Local Church*. Grand Rapids: Baker, 1991.

Van Gelder, Craig. *The Essence of the Church: A Community Created by the Spirit*. Grand Rapids, MI: Baker, 2000.

Van Gelder, Craig and Dwight J. Zscheile's *The Missional Church in Perspective: Mapping Trends and Shaping the Conversation*. Grand Rapids, MI: Baker Academic, 2011.

Vanhoozer, Kevin J., C. G. Bartholomew, D. J. Treier and N. T. Wright (eds.) *Dictionary for Theological Interpretation of the Bible*. Grand Rapids, MI: Baker Academic, 2005.

Van Rheenen, Gailyn. "A Theology of Culture: Desecularizing Anthropology." *International Journal of Frontier Missions* 14(1) 1997: 33-8.

Van Rheenen, Gailyn. "Transplanted and Contextualized Churches." Missology.org. *Monthly Missiological Reflection* #17. http://www.missiology.org/mr-17-transplanted-and-contextualized-churches/ (accessed 8th February 2016).

Vanhoozer, Kevin, C. A. Anderson and M.J. Sleasman (eds.) *Everyday Theology: How to Read Cultural Texts and Interpret Trends*. Grand Rapids, MI: Baker Academic, 2007.

Walls, Andrew F. "Converts for Proselytes? The Crisis over Conversion in the Early Church." *International Bulletin of Missionary Research* 28(1) 2004: 2-7.

Walls, Andrew F. "Old Athens and New Jerusalem: Some Signposts for Christian Scholarship in the Early History of Mission." *International Bulletin of Missionary Research* 21(4) 1997: 146-53.

Walls, Andrew F. "The Gospel as the Prisoner and Liberator of Culture." *Missionalia* 10 (3) 1982: 93-105.

Walls, Andrew F. *Missionary Movement in Christian History: Studies in the Transmission of Faith.* Maryknoll, N.Y.: Orbis, 1996.

Walsh, Brian and R. Middleton. *The Transforming Vision: Shaping a Christian Worldview.* Downers Grove, IL: Inter Varsity Press, 1984.

Wan, Enoch. "Practical Contextualization: A Case Study of Evangelising Contemporary Chinese." *Global Missiology* (Oct. 2003), http://ojs.globalmissiology.org/index.php/english/issue/view/27 (accessed 8th February 2016)

Whiteman, Darrell L. "Part I: Anthropology and Mission: the Incarnational Connection." *International Journal of Frontier Missions* 21(1) 2004: 34-45.

Whiteman, Darrell L. "Part II: Anthropology and Mission: the Incarnational Connection. *International Journal of Frontier Missions* 21(2) 2004: 78-89.

Whiteman, Darrell L. "Contextualization: the Theory, the Gap and the Challenge." *International Bulletin of Missionary Research* 21 (1) 1997: 2-7.

Wilkins, Michael. *Following the Master.* Grand Rapids, MI: Zondervan , 1992.

Winter, Ralph. "The Re-Amateurization of Missions." *Occasional Bulletin of the Evangelical Missiological Society* (Spring 1996), http://www.dake.com/EMS/bulletins/winter.htm (accessed 8th February 2016).

Wonsuk Ma and Julie C. Ma (editors). *Asian Church and God's Mission.* Manila, Philippines: OMF Literature & West Caldwell, N.J.: Mountain World Mission, 2003.

Zahniser, A.H. *Symbols and Ceremony: Making Disciples across Cultures.* Monrovia, CA: MARC, 1997.

LIST OF CONTRIBUTORS

Editors

Warren R. Beattie (*editor*) is the M.A. Programme Leader and Lecturer in Mission Studies teaching Contextual Theology, Arts with Mission and Research at All Nations Christian College, Hertfordshire, U.K. He has a Ph.D. in World Christianity from the Centre for the Study of World Christianity, New College, University of Edinburgh and is an ordained minister with the Church of Scotland. Formerly, he was Director for Mission Research at OMF International (IHQ) from 2006 - 2012 and editor of *Mission Round Table: the Occasional Bulletin of OMF Resarch*; a faculty member at the Discipleship Training Centre, Singapore, lecturing in Mission Studies (1998-2012); and, prior to that, worked in South Korea in missions' mobilization, leadership training and part-time lecturing at a Christian university. He has presented on Mission Studies in the Asia-Pacific region and in Europe and has written articles and contributed to books on mission including three volumes of the WEA Globalization of Mission Series – *One World or Many* (William Carey, 2003); *Global Missions* (William Carey, 2011) and *The Church in Mission* (William Carey, 2015 forthcoming) and to the *Dictionary of Mission Theology* (IVP, 2007).

Les Taylor (pseudonym) is a theologically trained anthropologist who has lived and worked in Muslim Southeast Asia since 2000. Since completing his Ph.D. in anthropology in 2009, he has held a range of research positions in local universities while also teaching intensive courses in theological seminaries. His principal academic interests are the history of religious change in Southeast Asia, the localisation of Islam, and modern Islamic movements. He is passionate about cross-cultural ambassadors and advocates being as familiar with the world of the religious other in their neighbourhood, as the word of God. His most recent missiological publications include a chapter in *Global Mission* (William Carey, 2011)]

David Harley served as the Principal of All Nations Christian College before being appointed as the General Director of OMF International. He was trained at the University of Cambridge and holds doctorates in missiology from Columbia International University (USA) and the University of Utrecht (Netherlands). David was the Lausanne Associate for Jewish Evangelism for nine years and has also worked in the UK, Ethiopia and Singapore. He has spoken at conferences, churches, Bible colleges and training schools in all five continents. He is the author of several books including *Missionary Training* (Boekencentrum, 2000) and *Preparing to Serve: Training for Cross-cultural Mission* (William Carey, 1995).

Daniel Daesoon Kim is currently serving as the Director of Chiang Mai Theological Seminary, while actively engaging in planting several community of believers in Thailand (with his wife Song), since they became members of OMF International in 1998. He has a degree in Biochemistry from UCLA, and M.Div. and M.Th. degrees from Talbot school of Theology of Biola University (USA). He is currently a candidate for a D. Miss. Programme at the School of Intercultural Studies at Biola University and has written several articles on contextualization and mission. Daniel has two grown children – Joshua and Hannah.

Phil Nicholson grew up in Sydney, Australia. He studied biochemistry and worked in medical research before being challenged to be involved in cross-cultural missions. After working as a youth pastor in a Chinese Australian church, and reaching out to overseas students, he went to serve in Taiwan with his wife, Irene. Phil has been living in Taiwan as an OMF missionary since 1992. In addition to a degree in science, he has an M.A. (Ministry) from the Australian College of Theology and has worked amongst university students with Campus Evangelical Fellowship in Taipei for over ten years, teaching the Bible and training students for ministry cross-culturally in Mandarin and English. He has a passion to teach God's word in a relevant way to help people to grow in their understanding of, and commitment, to Jesus Christ.

Minho Song served with OMF International in the Philippines as assistant professor of Missions at Asian Theological Seminary and teaching pastor of Diliman Campus Bible Church in Quezon City. He studied at the University of British Columbia (B.A.), Regent College (M.Div; Th.M.) and Trinity Evangelical Divinity School (Ph.D.). He is currently the senior pastor of Young Nak Korean Presbyterian Church of Toronto and is married with three daughters.

Melville Szto was born in Klang in Malaysia but grew up in Singapore. He studied for degrees in chemical engineering and theology in Australia. He met his wife Salome (from Indonesia) in Adelaide and they married when they returned to Singapore and Melville began teaching at Singapore Bible College. They joined OMF International in 1975, going to Japan where they have been involved in evangelism and church-planting in various cities in Hokkaido. From 1994 to 2002, Melville served as dean of the Asian Cross-Cultural Training Institute, in Singapore, training and preparing new missionaries for service in Asia. The Sztos then returned to church-planting work in Japan and retired, in 2010, and now serve in pastoral ministry at their church, Bethesda Frankel Estate Church and with the Japanese Christian Fellowship in Singapore. The Sztos have two children, born and raised in Japan, Sharon and Mark.

Brian Michell and his wife Lois joined OMF International in 1970 and have served in Indonesia, Malaysia and Singapore, working in theological education and mission leadership. Brian was the OMF Area Director for Malaysia and Singapore in the late 1970s through the early 1990s, and also deputized as Director of Overseas Ministries (now called International Director for Evangelization) for two years. His M.A. was in languages, literature and the social sciences; his M.Th. in practical training for ministry; and his D.Miss. in missionary development of and partnership with emerging national church leaders. He has taught Mission at Trinity Theological College, Singapore and now, though based in New Zealand in retirement, continues to teach in theological colleges in East Malaysia twice a year and to visit Timor Leste twice a year to help with pastoral training and church development projects.

Karen L.K. Quek (*layout editor*) is a graduate in English Literature from the National University of Singapore (1997). On graduation, she worked in the civil service, in the Prime Minister's Office, as part of the Public Service Division (Singapore) where she was involved in display, exhibition and media projects including the "PS21 website" and *Challenge* magazine. Karen joined OMF Singapore in 2000 working with OMF Books, responsible for the OMF Media website and *Go! Singapore.* Since 2005, she has been responsible for the graphic and layout editing of all the publishing projects of Mission Research Media – including the journal *Mission Round Table* (over twenty editions) and the electronic digest *Research Matters* (now in its sixth volume.)

MISSIONAL CHURCH IN ASIAN CONTEXTS – SERIES

The series *Missional Church in Asian Contexts* aims to help Christians to think afresh about the challenges that face the church in Asia:

> We are concerned with the **church** because we view local communities of Christians as the foundation and core of God's work in the world. All the themes addressed will be of relevance to the church and its communal life.

> We want to stress the **missional** character of the church because the church's task is to look inwards and outwards – inwards to build communities of the kingdom – but outwards to represent the kingdom to the whole of society and to present "good news" to others.

> We have an interest in **Asian contexts** because the local communities of Asia are found in many people groups and nations, and form a rich diversity of cultures which embrace more than 2 billion people across the face of the globe.

Against that backdrop, *Missional Church in Asian Contexts* seeks to show that the interplay between church and mission involves a dynamic, ongoing dialogue. We want to contribute to a robust understanding of "missional": a missional church is not just concerned with local contexts, but is a church that looks out to "the ends of the earth"; a missional church does not just empower local people, but is a church that partners with the global church.

The series *Missional Church in Asian Contexts* aims to show that theology for Asian contexts must connect to the local churches and their needs and aspirations. We include contributions that demonstrate a healthy balance between theory and practice: the pragmatism of the church-planter will be tempered by theological reflection and the ideas of the educators will be shaped by realities "on the ground." We hope that by drawing on writers from east and west, we can point the way to missional communities that partner in the work of the missional church in Asian contexts in the 21st century.

Mission Research Media

Mission Research Media is the publishing wing of the Mission Research Department of OMF International. It represents a number of colleagues who reflect together on the church in Asian contexts and seeks to produce a range of materials that help Christians engage in mission in creative ways.

Writers for Mission Research Media, who come both from Asia and from other parts of the world, have different vocational backgrounds but have all studied theology and mission, and have practical experience of working in Asian cultures.

Our publications deal with a wide range of topics and perspectives around the theme of the church in Asian contexts and we seek to stimulate creative thinking about mission in contemporary Asia.

Mission Research Media produces four different kinds of publications: the journal *Mission Round Table*; the electronic digest *Research Matters*; *Mission Research Guides* – booklets on writing and researching about mission like *Develop as a Writer*; and *Missional Church in Asian Contexts* – a series of books on mission and ministry.

Ministry across cultures: sharing the Christian faith in Asia is the first in a series of books which will look at important issues that affect the church and its mission in 21st century Asia.

For further information contact us at Int.Research@omfmail.com or visit our website at http://www.omf.org/about-omf/mission-research

MISSION RESEARCH MEDIA

Regnum Studies in Global Christianity

In the latter part of the twentieth century the world witnessed significant changes in global Christian dynamics. The Regnum Studies in Global Christianity series explores the issues with which the global church struggles, focusing in particular on ministry rooted in Africa, Asia, Latin America and Eastern Europe.

Not only does the series make available studies that will help the global church learn from past and present, it provides a platform for provocative and prophetic voices to speak to the future of Christianity. The editors and the publisher pray particularly that the series will grow as a public space, where the voices of church leaders from the majority world will contribute out of wisdom drawn from experience and reflection, thus shaping a healthy future for the global church. To this end, the editors invite theological seminaries and universities from around the world to submit relevant scholarly dissertations for possible publication in the series. Through this, it is hoped that the series will provide a forum for South-to-South as well as South-to-North dialogues.

Volumes in this series are printed in paperback, unless otherwise stated.

Jesus and the Resurrection
David Emmanuel Singh (Ed)
2014 / 978-1-870345-58-4 / 205pp
Our aim here is to build a bridge between Muslims and Christians with Jesus in the centre of the discourse. As an idea, 'resurrection' is shared by and is central to the eschatologies of Christianity, Islam and Judaism. In Islam, the belief in life after death, resurrection and the day of judgement are so central that they are considered to be one of its 'Five Pillars'. Life has meaning because in resurrection, humanity will meet its maker on the Day of Judgement.

Seeing New Facets of the Diamond
Gillian Mary Bediako, Benhardt Y Quarshie, Kwabena Asamoah-Gyadu (Eds)
2014 / 978-1-908355-59-1/ 378pp
In the five years since Kwame Bediako passed away there has been a growing desire among colleagues and friends to put together a book that would honour his memory. The title has been chosen to reflect the range of interests and concerns that motivated Bediako's scholarly work, including his founding and nurturing of ACI.

Bernhard Reitsma

The God of My Enemy:
The Middle East and the Nature of God

2014 / 978-1-908355-50-8 / 206pp

Bernhard Reitsma lived and worked among Christians in the Middle East for several years. He has shared their struggles and was challenged to reconsider different kinds of Israel theology. In this the core questions is whether the God of my enemy can also be my God. How can the God of the present State of Israel also be the God of the Palestinians?

Following Jesus: Journeys in Radical Discipleship – Essays in Honor of Ronald J Sider
Paul Alexander and Al Tizon (Eds)

2013 / 978-1-908355-27-0 / 235pp

Ronald J. Sider and the organization that he founded, Evangelicals for Social Action, are most respected for their pioneering work in evangelical social concern. However, Sider's great contribution to social justice is part of a larger vision – biblical discipleship. This book brings together a group of scholar-activists, old and young, to reflect upon theradical implications for the 21st century.

Relectuant or Radical Revolutionaries?
Cawley Bolt

2013 / 978-1-908355-18-8 / 287pp

This study is based on extensive research that challenges traditional ways of understanding some evangelical missionaries of nineteenth century Jamaica and calls for revision of those views. It highlights the strength and character of persons facing various challenges of life in their effort to be faithful to the guiding principles of their existence.

Contemporary Pentecostal Christianity:
Interpretations from an African Context

2013 / 978-1-908355-07-2 / 194pp

J Kwabena Asamoah-Gyada

Pentecostalism is the fastest growing stream of Christianity in the world. The real evidence for the significance of Pentecostalism lies in the actual churches they have built and the numbers they attract. This work interprets key theological and missiological themes in African Pentecostalism by using material from the live experiences of the movement itself.

For the full listing, visit www.ocms.ac.uk/regnum